EYE ON
Art

CUBISM

by Cynthia J. Mines

LUCENT BOOKS

An imprint of Thomson Gale, a part of The Thomson Corporation

Union Public Library
1980 Morris Avenue
Union, N.J. 07083

THOMSON

GALE

Detroit • New York • San Francisco • New Haven, Conn. • Waterville, Maine • London

LIBRARY OF CONGRESS CATALOGING-IN-PUBLICATION DATA

Mines, Cynthia J.
  Cubism / by Cynthia J. Mines.
    p. cm. — (Eye on art)
  Includes bibliographical references and index.
  ISBN-13: 978-1-59018-961-0 (hard cover : alk. paper)
  ISBN-10: 1-59018-961-2 (hard cover : alk. paper)
  1. Cubism—Juvenile literature. I. Title. II. Series.
  N6494.C8M56 2006
  709'.04'032—dc22
                                                          2006012931

Printed in the United States of America

CONTENTS

Foreword

"Art has no other purpose than to brush aside . . . everything that veils reality from us in order to bring us face to face with reality itself."

—French philosopher Henri-Louis Bergson

Some thirty-one thousand years ago, early humans painted strikingly sophisticated images of horses, bison, rhinoceroses, bears, and other animals on the walls of a cave in southern France. The meaning of these elaborate pictures is unknown, although some experts speculate that they held ceremonial significance. Regardless of their intended purpose, the Chauvet-Pont-d'Arc cave paintings represent some of the first known expressions of the artistic impulse.

From the Paleolithic era to the present day, human beings have continued to create works of visual art. Artists have developed painting, drawing, sculpture, engraving, and many other techniques to produce visual representations of landscapes, the human form, religious and historical events, and countless other subjects. The artistic impulse also finds expression in glass, jewelry, and new forms inspired by new technology. Indeed, judging by humanity's prolific artistic output throughout history, one must conclude that the compulsion to produce art is an inherent aspect of being human, and the results are among humanity's greatest cultural achievements: masterpieces such as the architectural marvels of ancient Greece, Michelangelo's perfectly rendered statue *David*, Vincent van Gogh's visionary painting *Starry Night*, and endless other treasures.

The creative impulse serves many purposes for society. At its most basic level, art is a form of entertainment or the means

Introduction

A Revolution in Art

When the art movement known as Cubism shattered the traditions of realistic, or representative, art in the first decade of the twentieth century, it reflected a European society that had itself undergone radical change in recent decades. Especially in the cities, the Industrial Revolution of the 1800s had produced marvels—electricity in houses and streets, moving pictures, suspension bridges—and European artists were eager to experience the new excitement of urban life. Paris, always an artistic center, was a particularly exciting place to be at the dawn of the twentieth century, as art, music, architecture, and literature flourished alongside the great scientific and technological advances. In Paris this period of invention and cultural achievement, from the late 1800s to World War I, was viewed as a golden age and given its own label: the Belle Époque, or "beautiful era."

In this climate of dramatic social and technological change, many Belle Époque artists were inspired to find new ways of looking at the world and innovative techniques to depict it. The most radical of these artists were the Cubists, mostly painters who intellectually tore their subject matter into pieces—geometric shapes such as planes, diamonds, and cubes—and then reassembled them in subjective ways on canvas. Their ideas and works departed drastically from centuries-old painterly ideals: Traditionally, art was judged by its ability to objectively, accurately, and realistically depict its subject. In sharp contrast, the Cubists produced distorted images that sometimes gave viewers the sensation of looking at a painting through shattered glass.

Art professor, curator, and authority on twentieth-century art Robert Rosenblum summarizes the significance of the Cubists' break with tradition: "The genesis of this new style, which was to alter the entire course of Western painting, sculpture, and even architecture, produced one of the most exhilarating moments in the history of art."[1] Most art historians agree that art, and the standards by which it is judged, changed more in the first decade of the twentieth century than it had in the previous five centuries.

Impressionist painter Camille Pissarro depicts a Parisian scene in his 1897 work *Boulevard Montmartre: Morning, Gray Weather.* A few years later, Paris would become a hotbed of artistic innovation.

But this does not mean that Cubism was eagerly accepted by the art establishment or the general public. Like many other unsettling changes, Cubism was variously viewed as groundbreaking and shocking, great and awful, and attracted both supporters and opponents. The controversy was centered in Paris.

Life in Belle Époque Paris

Turn-of-the-century events gave Parisians much to talk about as they gathered in cafés along the city's wide boulevards. In the

Brilliantly lit in this photo, the controversial Eiffel Tower was the centerpiece of the 1900 World's Fair in Paris.

United States the Wright brothers were experimenting with flight, and the German-Swiss physicist Albert Einstein had just published his theory of relativity. At home the Eiffel Tower, constructed more than a decade earlier, remained a subject of great controversy. The towering structure had been built for the 1889 Paris World's Fair by French engineer Alexandre-Gustave Eiffel to demonstrate how steel and iron could be used to erect tall structures. By 1900, millions had visited Paris just to see it. But many Parisians considered it a monstrosity and an assault on the ideals of grace and form in architecture. Some thought it such an eyesore they demanded it be torn down.

In planning the 1900 World's Fair, Paris officials again made the Eiffel Tower the centerpiece of the international exposition. Fifty million people—including a talented young Spanish artist named Pablo Picasso—celebrated the birth of a new century by traveling to Paris to see the much-debated Eiffel Tower and the grand art palaces built just for the World's Fair. Four years after his first visit, Picasso settled permanently in the low-rent Montmartre district of Paris, home to many struggling artists. In 1907 he met the French painter Georges Braque, and together they embarked on a series of artistic explorations that evolved into the movement known as Cubism. Like the Eiffel Tower, Cubist artworks emerged from controversy to become recognized worldwide as icons of the modern age. Art historian David Cottington calls Cubism "the most seminal movement for the history of Modernism in all the arts."[2]

Conquering Form and Space

The word *cubes* was first used in reference to this new kind of art in a review that appeared (next to an article about Wilbur Wright's experiments with flight) in the November 14, 1908, edition of the French magazine *Gil Blas*. Just as humans were attempting to defy gravity by flying heavier-than-air craft and building sky-scraping steel structures, innovative artists were trying to conquer space in their own way. A particular concern of the emerging Cubists was how to translate three-dimensional reality onto a two-dimensional canvas, and so they were particularly interested in Einstein's discussion of the three dimensions of space—height, width, and depth. When Einstein's theory addressed a fourth dimension—time—it ignited the imaginations of the artists who were experimenting with geometric shapes to represent space and matter.

Most ordinary Parisians were unaware of the Cubist experiments until a famous Paris exhibition in 1910. For the next four years, until France entered World War I, Cubism both flourished and gave rise to another artistic invention—collage. Again reflecting the shattered society of war-torn Europe, Cubist painters literally turned reality upside down and inside out. Art—and the world—never again looked the same after the invention of Cubism.

Rebelling Against Tradition: The Precursors of Cubism

Cubism revolutionized art because it abandoned the tradition of realistically depicting the subject of a painting. For centuries, the goal of artists had been to represent a subject as accurately and in as much detail as possible. The Cubists, by contrast, wanted to create a whole new way of painting. To do this, they analyzed the appearance of a subject, then cut that view up into pieces and reassembled them in a way that made sense to them but not necessarily to the viewer. This method often produced bizarre-looking people and scenes that horrified art critics and the public. The artists, however, believed this approach produced a truer picture of reality than more representational art because it reflected the deeper perceptions of the mind, not just the eyes.

Because Cubism took a decisive step away from realism toward abstraction, the movement is often considered the beginning of modern art. Art historians disagree, however, on exactly when the movement started. The creation of this new kind of art—which included the invention of collage—evolved over several years, propelled by various forces that came together in Paris in the early 1900s. Though a definitive

Cubist style was not identifiable until 1908, the seeds were planted well before the turn of the century.

The Cubists were part of a group of cutting-edge Parisian artists and writers who were a step ahead of public taste. They became known as the avant-garde, a French military term meaning "advance guard" that gave rise to its English equivalent, *vanguard*. It was an apt description for the progressive artists and writers who moved ahead of the rest of society in exploring new ground.

A Break with the Past

The avant-garde artists infuriated the French officials who controlled government-sponsored art exhibitions because they seemed to have a total disregard for artistic tradition. Art had been judged by its realism and a stiff set of technical standards —the ability to show precise detail but no visible brushstrokes, for example—since the fifteenth century. In 1648 French King Louis XIV founded the Royal Academy of Painting and Sculpture to train talented students and cultivate masters capable of carrying out royal commissions. Various royal academies were combined in the early 1800s to form the Académie des Beaux-Arts (Academy of Fine Arts), which oversaw art contests known as salons at which graduates displayed their work and vied for medals. Juries selected works for the annual, government-sponsored Salon de Paris; acceptance to this prestigious salon was essential for any artist who wanted recognition or success in France.

Academy officials believed the only acceptable subjects for public exhibition were religious scenes, portraits, mythology, historical events, landscapes, and still lifes. They also expected artists to use subdued colors and a classical approach that favored symmetry and formal composition. Without question, the works were to accurately depict their subject matter; the best works were judged to be those whose details were so realistic they looked much like a modern photograph.

These guidelines were still in effect in the mid-1800s, when Paris became the artistic capital of Europe, its grand museums and large, prestigious public art exhibitions attracting some twelve thousand artists to the city. Works selected for display in the Paris salons were seen by tens of thousands of people and perhaps purchased by future patrons, and salon artists were eligible to win cash prizes and commissions for more work. To be accepted, however, artists had to comply with the strict guidelines set forth by the Academy.

In the 1850s a few artists living in Paris began to rebel against these long-held artistic traditions. After the invention of the camera in 1839, some artists no longer felt compelled to meticulously record a subject or scene for posterity because the new device could do so much more easily. Artists therefore felt freer to experiment with broader and more fluid brushstrokes, and some did not even attempt to represent scenes accurately. Artists also ventured outdoors to paint scenes under varying conditions of natural light. Because these paintings represented a shifting impression rather than a realistic depiction, the artists became known as Impressionists.

Cubism: Reinventing Art

Eighteenth-century French artist Jean-Baptiste Greuze used his wife as the model for his painting *La Laitière*, or *The Milkmaid*.

Although *not* a Cubist painting, the work below shows a playful artist's attempt to add a few Cubist elements to Greuze's painting.

Traditional painting had been realistic and highly detailed.

Artistic conventions of symmetry and formal composition were the rule.

An artist's ability to show precise detail with no visible brushstrokes was highly regarded.

In *actual* Cubist works, artists broke up their subject matter into fragments, analyzed it, and reassembled it.

Their paintings were abstract—intentionally distorted and full of sharp planes and geometric shapes.

To capture the essence of a subject, Cubists typically presented it from many points of view simultaneously.

Led by Edouard Manet, this new generation of artists appreciated shapes and colors more than faithful depictions of their subject matter. They painted not only what the eye could see but what they felt, and believed this style better conveyed the excitement, color, and diversity of Paris in the last half of the nineteenth century.

Though the Impressionists' subjects were still recognizable, these artists took a significant step away from realism. The salon juries considered this a radical departure and were appalled. Besides deriding the style in which the Impressionists painted, the juries also objected to their subject matter, which tended to be common people and everyday items rather than pastoral landscapes, historic events, or important people. This was shocking to the French art establishment, which did not consider, for example, a lowly dancer or circus performer, or even a gathering of middle-class Parisians enjoying a picnic, subjects worthy of art.

Like other Impressionists, Edouard Manet emphasized color and shape rather than strict realism in his work, as evident in his *Open-Air Cabaret.*

As a result, the avant-garde works were consistently rejected by the Paris salons. Manet's first salon submission was an 1859 painting titled *The Absinthe Drinker*, a somber study of a drunken man down on his luck. The judges emphatically rejected it, offended by its dark subject matter. A painting Manet completed in 1862, *Music in the Tuileries Gardens*, did not fare any better. The French art establishment attacked the painting's sketchy style and lack of detail, as well as its subject, ordinary middle-class citizens listening to music in a park near the Louvre museum.

The cultural war between the avant-garde artists and the French art establishment reached its peak in 1863, when the Salon de Paris jury rejected two thousand of the five thousand paintings submitted that year. Faced with a massive protest, Emperor Napoléon III granted the Academy independence from government oversight, changed its name to the École des Beaux-Arts, and decided to open a second exhibition, the Salon des Refusés (Salon of the Refused), for artists whose works had been rejected. When the Salon des Refusés opened on May 17, 1863, thousands of spectators flocked to see the works. They came primarily out of curiosity, however, and most jeered the works on display, many of which were admittedly bad and deserved the jury's rejection. Yet though the public reaction was generally hostile, artists took note of the best of the new works on display, and the rebellion against realistic painting gained momentum.

The Impressionists' Debut

Faced with continued rejection by the salons, a group of Impressionists took a bold step in 1874 and decided to organize their own exhibition. It was a risky financial venture, but they needed a way to reach potential buyers for their art. The exhibition of works by twenty-nine artists was held in a photographer's studio because no gallery would show their work. The artists were unprepared for the scorn the exhibition received from both critics and the public. Critics assailed the painting's blurred details, lack of outline, bright colors, and broad brushstrokes.

Salon judges found Manet's brooding painting *The Absinthe Drinker* offensive.

The artists persevered, however, holding another group exhibition in 1876 and six more over the next decade. Eventually, avant-garde artists sought other venues in which they could exhibit their work. The resulting Salon des Indépendants (Salon of the Independents) organized exhibitions every spring beginning in 1884, and the Salon d'Automne (Autumn Salon) began in 1903. Though these two salons were not quite as rigid as the official Salon de Paris, the juries still tended to be conservative in choosing what they felt was appropriate for public consumption.

The Wild Beasts

The Salon d'Automne found itself at the center of a huge public scandal in 1905 when it allowed a group of avant-garde artists led by French painter Henri Matisse to exhibit. Matisse had studied at the official art school of the Academy, but eventually rebelled against the school's traditional approach. He began using brilliant colors and clearly defined shapes with no shading. His use of large, unbroken blocks of color was even more radical than the Impressionists' sweeping brushstrokes of color.

Matisse and his group unveiled this new style of painting at the 1905 Salon d'Automne. The exhibition displayed the boldest, most brightly colored paintings yet seen in Paris, and the art establishment was incensed by the artists' flagrant disregard for realism. Critics attacked this experimental art in newspapers and journals. One art critic, Louis Vauxcelles,

Montmartre, a hilltop district overlooking Paris, had become known as the epicenter of the art world by the end of the nineteenth century. Cheap rents began attracting artists to the area in the 1830s. More than five hundred artists settled there between 1860 and 1910, creating a vast district of studios. Several artists, including Pablo Picasso, lived and worked in a dilapidated group of buildings known as Bateau-Lavoir.

After the sun set and they could no longer see to paint, the artists gathered in Montmartre's many cafés and cabarets to discuss new ideas in art, literature, technology, politics, and philosophy. It was here that the Impressionists' first exhibition was planned and that the tenets of Fauvism and Cubism were first dissected and debated. Three of Montmartre's most popular gathering places for artists—Le Lapin Agile, Chat Noir, and Moulin Rouge—were frequently depicted in their works.

A May 1898 poster advertises the Chat Noir (Black Cat) café, a favorite gathering spot for avant-garde artists.

referred to the artists as *fauves* (wild beasts) in his review. Though Vauxcelles had used the term as an insult, the artists cheerfully adopted the name.

The Fauves favored flat compositions with even less detail than the Impressionists. The result was a still greater departure from reality. Moreover, while Impressionist paintings often featured delicate, subtle use of pastels and shades of light, the Fauves preferred bolder and more exuberant colors, simplified lines, and almost no gradations of color. This caused some of their paintings to resemble pages from a coloring book. The Fauves thought this daring approach was a better way to express the vividness and excitement of Paris. Their goal was to express joy through the spontaneous use of bright—sometimes clashing—colors and bold, clearly defined figures. For instance, a portrait Matisse painted of his wife used red-orange and violet on a bright green background.

Though it was short-lived—by 1908 Matisse was moving toward a more decorative and formal style—Fauvism was the first major art movement of the new century and an important bridge between Impressionism and Cubism. In addition to Matisse, artists associated with the Fauves such as André Derain, Raoul Dufy, and Maurice de Vlaminck would figure prominently in the even more radical art soon to emerge in France.

The Influence of Cézanne

Matisse and other artists working in Paris early in the twentieth century were greatly influenced by Paul Cézanne, another French artist who had exhibited with the Impressionists but then began to pursue his own unique style. Born in 1839 to an affluent family in Aix-en-Provence in the south of France, Cézanne moved to Paris when he was twenty-two to pursue his dream of becoming a painter. Through the Caribbean-born Impressionist painter Camille Pissarro, Cézanne met Manet, whose works he had admired. For the next several years Cézanne split his time between Paris and his provincial home, where the local art gallery considered his often dark, brooding paintings too radical to exhibit.

As artist Paul Cézanne's style evolved, he began breaking down images into geometric shapes, as shown in his work *In the Park at Château Noir.*

Cézanne submitted works to the official Salon from 1864 to 1869, but they were consistently rejected. Then he exhibited with the Impressionists at their first show in 1874, but he found their style lacking in form and began to distance himself from them.

When Cézanne found he could not satisfactorily reproduce on canvas what he saw in nature, he became obsessed with finding a way to overcome the canvas's two-dimensional limitations. In the 1880s he began breaking down images into geometric shapes and experimenting with space and depth. He used muted colors so they would not interfere with his study of a subject's structure, and began a lifelong fascination with a mountain near his home, Mont Saint-Victoire, which he painted more than sixty times trying to capture the firmness and solidity he felt was lacking in the Impressionists' work.

Cézanne also experimented with perspective. Traditionally, painters produced artwork with a single, consistent perspective, or viewpoint, but Cézanne sometimes viewed a subject from more than one perspective in the same painting. In his *Still Life with Apples and Oranges* (c. 1895–1900), for instance, he depicted the apples from above and the oranges from the side. He experimented with perspective by breaking down a subject into planes, which he arranged at various angles to each other. He also distorted the shapes of objects and figures, and attempted to create movement in his paintings by using subtle transitions of tone and color. He was more interested in exploring visual and psychological effects than in realism.

The Birth of Modern Art

Because the reclusive Cézanne tended to work in isolation outside Paris, his experiments were not widely known during his lifetime. He was ignored by the art establishment, and major exhibitions of his work were mounted only after his death in 1906. In retrospect, many critics point to the paintings he created from 1900 to 1905 as the point at which modern art was born; indeed, Cézanne is often referred to as the father of modern art. He skillfully portrayed the underlying geometric forms found in nature, and by using color planes was able to create paintings with a sense of three dimensions. An example is a series of innovative paintings called *The Great Bathers*, which he worked on during the last years of his life. In them, Cézanne's nude female figures are jagged and distorted: Their limbs form parallel lines and trees in the background lean toward the center like two sides of a triangle.

Although Cézanne had no way of knowing it, his use of structure, geometrical composition, and balance paved the way for the founding of Cubism. A comment he made in 1904 that was quoted in the French literary gazette *Mercure de France*—"Treat nature in terms of the cylinder, the sphere, and the cone"[3]—was later cited by Cubism historians as prophetic.

In 1907 the Salon d'Automne dedicated a retrospective exhibition to Cézanne. The fifty-six paintings posthumously shown there clearly illustrated the progression toward his goal of making Impressionism, as he put it, "something solid and durable, like the art of the museums."[4]

The paintings also made a huge impression on visiting artists, including a young Spanish artist named Pablo Picasso, who had relocated permanently to Paris from Barcelona in 1904. At the time of his move, Picasso was painting in what later became known as his Blue Period, which had begun in 1901 after the suicide of his longtime friend Carlos Casagemas. During this period, Picasso's paintings were melancholy and often depicted lonely people. Because no one wanted to buy such solemn paintings, Picasso remained poor. The walls of his studio in the low-rent Montmartre district, where he lived and worked, were so thin his tea froze if left out in a cup overnight. All of the residents of the Bateau-Lavoir buildings where he lived had to share a single water spigot.

Perhaps because he identified with them, Picasso found inspiration in the downtrodden inhabitants of Montmartre, especially in its seedy cabarets and circuses. One of his favorite subjects was the Cirque Medrano and its performers. The

Cézanne's painting *Large Bathers II* exhibits his use of structural and geometrical composition, a style that later influenced Cubism.

Pablo Ruiz Picasso was born October 25, 1881, in Malaga, a coastal town in southern Spain. His father was a painter, drawing teacher, and curator of the town's museum. A child prodigy, Pablo was drawing almost before he could talk and had mastered oil painting by the time he was thirteen. When he was fourteen, his family moved from the countryside to Barcelona, a cosmopolitan center in northern Spain, where he was admitted to advanced classes at the Royal Academy of Art. He rejected academic study, however, and preferred to congregate with other artists and writers at the Els Quatre Gats tavern to discuss important issues of the day.

The young intellectuals' favorite topic was Paris, the art capital of Europe. News of the approaching Exposition Universelle (World's Fair) whetted Picasso's appetite even more to visit the famous city, and when one

of his paintings was accepted for the exposition, he made plans to visit. In October 1900, at the age of nineteen, Picasso set out for Paris with an artist friend, Carlos Casagemas. By day Picasso toured the Louvre and other great museums. By night he found inspiration in the city's cafés, cabarets, and circuses, and absorbed everything he saw. He visited Paris several times before settling permanently in the Montmartre district in 1904.

Picasso poses on a street in Montmartre in about 1904.

harlequins and clowns he painted, however, were not generally depicted as happy, but as sad or dejected. This did not change even after he entered his so-called Rose Period, when his paintings began to feature more pink than blue tints. An example was the large 1905 canvas titled *The Family of Saltimbanques* (circus performers), which depicted a vagabond troop of unsmiling performers set in a lonely, barren landscape.

Fortunate Meetings

Picasso's fortunes began to change in 1905, the year he painted *The Family of Saltimbanques*. That winter brother and sister Leo Stein and Gertrude Stein, expatriate Americans who had become interested in modern art movements since moving to Paris in 1903, viewed some of his harlequin paintings in a gallery owned by Clovis Sagot. They bought one called *The Acrobat's Family with a Monkey*, and were so taken by Picasso's work that they asked to meet him. When the Steins made their first visit to the artist's studio in the Bateau-Lavoir, they bought several additional paintings for more than eight hundred francs, a huge sum at the time.

Leo Stein, an art critic and painter himself, and Gertrude Stein, a poet and eventual champion of modernist literature, played a crucial role in Picasso's success as an artist. Gertrude became a friend and patron to Picasso and other Parisian artists, buying and covering her apartment walls with their work. She also hosted weekly gatherings of artists and writers at her home. Stein became Picasso's subject in 1905, when he began a portrait of her that took ninety sittings and more than a year to complete. The famously masklike face and bulky body in this portrait are regarded as foreshadows of the Cubist style he would soon pioneer.

In 1907, two years after the Steins met Picasso, another fateful meeting took place: The poet and art critic Guillaume Apollinaire introduced Picasso to Georges Braque, who had moved to Paris in 1900 to study the Impressionists but ended up being drawn instead to the Fauves. Braque had met Apollinaire through German art dealer Daniel-Henri

Kahnweiler, a friend and supporter of Picasso who had recently opened a gallery in Paris.

The two artists were about the same age: Picasso was born in 1881 in a small town in Spain, and Braque was born in a Paris suburb in 1882. However, Braque was still working as a house painter when Picasso established his own art studio in Barcelona. When the two met in Paris, Picasso was enjoying some financial success from his art, while Braque was still a relative newcomer to painting. Nevertheless, the pair quickly formed a friendship and a close working relationship.

The meeting with Picasso gave Braque the opportunity to be one of the first to see a canvas Picasso had been laboring over for more than a year. Picasso was very protective of his art and allowed few into his studio to see works in progress. When he did have visitors to his tiny living and studio quarters, he turned his paintings toward the wall so they could not be seen.

The painting Picasso showed Braque scandalized the French art world when it was privately shown in 1907. Even the most avant-garde artists were shocked by its form and subject matter—five grotesquely depicted naked prostitutes in a brothel, filling a canvas 8 feet by 7 feet, 8 inches (2.4m by 2.36m).

In the massive canvas, Picasso combined the techniques Cézanne had used to paint his famous series of bathers with shapes and images influenced by his own study of African art, in which he had developed an interest. The controversial painting, later named *Les Demoiselles d'Avignon* (*The Young Women of Avignon*, a Barcelona street), appeared to sever all ties with reality by depicting the women in a brutal way, with lopsided eyes, in erotic poses. In the painting Picasso deliberately distorted proportions and filled the composition with sharp planes, contradictory points of view and harsh colors. The jagged and distorted edges of the figures gave the impression of shards of broken glass. Even Matisse, who had shocked Paris with his Fauvist paintings, was alarmed by the turn Picasso's work had taken.

Others who saw the painting were even more horrified by the threatening appearance of two female figures who seemed

to be wearing primitive masks. Picasso had chosen African tribal mask imagery for its power and beauty, but most people saw the masks as frightening, violent symbols and could not comprehend their use in a painting of women. The art dealer Ambroise Vollard pronounced the painting the "work of a madman."[5] The authors of a history of the Montmartre art district summarize its reception: "In 1907, for the majority of people in Montmartre artistic circles, Picasso had quite simply murdered painting."[6]

But while most people condemned *Les Demoiselles*, Braque was intrigued by the path Picasso was blazing. He described *Les Demoiselles* admiringly as if "someone had drunk kerosene to spit fire."[7]

Others eventually appreciated the radically new work, and many contemporary art historians point to this canvas as the most important painting of the twentieth century. Because the painting was deemed too scandalous to display publicly for a decade, some historians argue that its immediate influence must have been limited, but *Les Demoiselles* is nevertheless widely accepted as the signal of a new art movement and a giant step toward modern art. That movement would become known as Cubism.

In 1907 those who saw Picasso's *Les Demoiselles d'Avignon* —on view here at a 2004 exhibit in New York City—found it incomprehensible and vulgar.

The Pioneers of Cubism: Picasso and Braque

Unbeknownst to each other, Picasso and Braque had both been heavily influenced by the Cézanne retrospective of 1907, and their artistic experiments beginning that autumn took a similar direction. In studying Cézanne's work, the two artists found some clues to a challenge that intrigued both of them: how to translate a complex three-dimensional reality onto a two-dimensional canvas.

The winter after they met, Braque began moving away from the bright colors of Fauvism and began to experiment with combining Cézanne's use of geometric structure with the simple shapes and sharp edges found in primitive art and African masks. At the same time, Picasso continued to explore the masklike shapes he had used in *Les Demoiselles* in another large painting of female figures, called *Three Women*.

Though the two artists were separated by several hundred miles during much of 1908, their work moved along remarkably parallel paths. In the spring of that year, Braque traveled to L'Estaque, a Mediterranean fishing village that was a favorite painting ground of Cézanne's. There he experimented with reducing landscapes and buildings to their essential components, which often appeared as cubelike shapes. In August

1908 Picasso traveled to a village near Creil in far northern France, where he too painted figures and landscapes using geometric shapes.

When the artists returned to Paris and compared their summer's work, the similarities were surprising. Two paintings, both completed in August 1908, bore startling likenesses in subject, composition, color, and structure. Braque's *Houses at L'Estaque* featured hatched brushwork and simplified geometric shapes; Picasso's *Cottage and Trees* had very similar subject matter and shapes, but pushed the use of varying perspectives further. Both paintings used a palette of muted greens and browns.

Although Braque and Picasso worked separately, Braque's work *Houses at L'Estaque* (pictured) was strikingly similar to a Picasso painting of the same time period.

The Movement Gets a Name

Braque was so pleased with his summer's work at L'Estaque that he entered several of his landscapes in the Salon d'Automne of 1908. While the salon jury was deliberating, the art critic Vauxcelles reported that juror Matisse had told him that "Braque has just sent a painting made of small cubes."[8]

Ultimately the jury rejected all but two of Braque's paintings. The artist then decided that rather than exhibit only two at the salon, he would show the entire series of thirty paintings

This 1909 photograph, shot by Picasso, shows Braque during a visit to Picasso's studio.

at Kahnweiler's art gallery in November. In a review of this show, published in the magazine *Gil Blas*, Vauxcelles wrote about Braque's painting *Houses at L'Estaque*, "He reduces everything, places, figures and houses, to geometrical schemes, to cubes."[9] Thus the new artistic form pioneered by Braque and Picasso was recognizable by the close of 1908—and the word used by Matisse and Vauxcelles stuck. The new style was called Cubism.

Artistic Dialogue

The dialogue between Braque and Picasso beginning in the late fall of 1908 is the most often-cited factor in the creation of Cubism. Their discussions spawned new ideas, and each artist was able to build on the experiments of the other. They had no idea they were creating a new kind of art. As Picasso later recalled: "When we made cubism, we had no intention of making cubism, we were only expressing what was within us."[10]

Given their very different backgrounds and temperaments, the close relationship between Braque and Picasso was unlikely. The patient, even-tempered Braque meticulously studied Cézanne's construction techniques, for example, while the explosive and temperamental Picasso intuitively forged ahead with his own experiments. Yet even though the two artists were occasionally at odds, the discussion was "always quick to bear fruit for both of us. . . . It was a union based on the independence of each,"[11] according to Braque.

Such camaraderie with another artist was particularly uncharacteristic of Picasso, who did not consider other artists his equal. Picasso, who lived to be ninety-two, produced thousands of works in many different styles, but according to biographer William Rubin, it was only during the Cubism phase that he showed "more than a passing involvement with the work of another artist."[12]

Because Braque and Picasso purposely worked in isolation from other artists, little is recorded of their artistic discussions. Few letters between them have survived, and they rarely discussed their work with others. There is evidence, however, that

GEORGES BRAQUE'S SEARCH FOR BEAUTY

Georges Braque was born on May 13, 1881, in Argenteuil, a Paris suburb by the Seine River, and moved with his family to Le Havre in 1890. His father convinced him to join the family's house-painting business in 1899. After moving to Paris, Braque experimented with different styles of painting, including Fauvism, in an attempt to depict true reality in his work.

He expressed his frustration in a 1910 interview with the Architectural Record:

Icould not represent a woman in all her natural beauty. . . . I do not have the skill. No one does. I must therefore create a new sort of beauty, the beauty which appears to me in terms of volume, line, mass and weight, and through that beauty I interpret my subjective impression. Nature is a mere pretext for a decorative composition, plus feeling. It suggests the emotion and I translate that emotion into art.

Quoted in Pierre Daix, *Cubists and Cubism.* New York: Rizzoli, 1982, p. 39.

the two consulted daily to test ideas and compare paintings. Forty years later Picasso recalled to a friend: "Almost every evening, either I went to Braque's studio or Braque came to mine. Each of us *had* to see what the other had done during the day."[13]

In March 1909, a few months after his collaboration with Picasso began, Braque exhibited work in the Salon des Indépendants. It would be his last appearance in a salon for a decade. In response to Braque's work, Vauxcelles again mocked the artist's "cubic oddities," describing them as "hardly intelligible."[14]

The reaction among viewers was not, however, uniformly negative. Also writing of Braque's work displayed in the Salon des Indépendants, critic André Salmon referred to the artist's "eloquent lines" and stated, "We owe him some noble discoveries."[15] This salon exhibition also prompted the first use of the word *cubism* in print. It appeared in the April 16, 1909, edition of the *Mercure de France* in an article about Braque, written by critic and poet Charles Morice.

Unlike Braque, Picasso never exhibited his work in the salons, thanks largely to his dealer friend Kahnweiler. In addition to displaying Picasso's work in his gallery, the art dealer early sensed the value of the artist's paintings and bought as many of them as he could afford. Starting in the spring of 1909, Kahnweiler attempted to buy almost everything both Braque and Picasso produced, a financial gamble but a major vote of confidence for the artists. Though he paid much more for Picasso's paintings than for Braque's, the arrangement gave both artists enough financial security to allow them to concentrate on experimental art rather than creating paintings that were palatable to the general buying public. Even so, while Picasso was able to move to larger quarters, Braque often had to write Kahnweiler and ask for help to pay his rent. Ultimately, Kahnweiler persuaded the two artists to sign exclusive contracts with him to sell their work. Thus it was to his advantage that their work be displayed solely in his gallery, and he discouraged them from participating in the public salons.

The Ghost of Cézanne

The paintings that hung in Kahnweiler's gallery reflected Braque's serious investigation of Cézanne's approach to structure and his efforts to integrate the solidity and formal organization of classical works with geometric fragmentation. Braque's compositions were generally orderly arrangements of objects separated from one another by overlapping shapes with indistinct boundaries. His palette was muted—mostly dull greens, ochres, black, and grays, neutral colors that did not distract the eye from the shapes and lines defining objects. He also used multiple viewpoints and inconsistent light sources to define the planes within a painting. He went beyond Cézanne when he totally excluded the skyline in his landscapes.

At this point, Picasso had less regard than either Cézanne or Braque for the order and harmony of classical art, but he eventually followed Braque in exploring Cézanne's approach to structure. Both painters also investigated Cézanne's device of "passage"—the use of parallel short, hatched strokes of paint, often in diamond-shaped patches, to soften edges or show transition. While Braque used the technique in a subtle way in his L'Estaque landscapes. Picasso's use was more obvious and purposely called attention to the device.

Analytic Cubism

Before long Braque moved beyond landscapes based on Cézanne's work toward a purer Cubist form, as did Picasso. In Cubist work before 1910, the subject of a picture was recognizable even though it might be distorted or broken into pieces. By contrast, works done between late 1909 and 1912 are often referred to as Analytic Cubism because the artists' dissection, analysis, and reassembly of their subjects became more pronounced, resulting in paintings whose subjects were much less identifiable to the observer. During this phase, Picasso and Braque so abstracted their works that the subjects were reduced to a series of overlapping planes and facets. In *The Guitarist*, for example, painted in 1910, Picasso reached the edge of abstraction with a canvas of brown and green lines that barely suggested the disconnected outline of a human form.

Because Picasso and Braque believed their reassembled versions of subjects more accurately reflected what the mind (rather than the eyes) perceived as the subject existed in space and over time, Cubism became known as an intellectual, rather than emotional or realistic, approach to art. Thus the label Analytic Cubism underscored this intellectual philosophy. Some art critics refer to this period as High Cubism because they consider it the time when Cubist exploration reached its purest expression. The period is sometimes also referred to as Hermetic Cubism because many paintings were so abstract their subject was decipherable only to the artists.

No matter what the period is called, Picasso's and Braque's artistic process from 1910 to 1912 followed this sequence: Before beginning a painting, the artists made many sketches so they could analyze the subject in great detail and from many angles. They broke the subject down into a multitude of smaller, geometrically shaped pieces. Then they combined the pieces, painted in sometimes radical rearrangement, on canvas. The use of facets and planes allowed them to show objects and people from many different angles at the same time.

Since the goal of Analytic Cubism was to examine form and space, the artists generally rejected all color but black, browns, and off-whites. Picasso tried using color during the Analytic phase but always painted it out because

Picasso's highly abstract pen and ink work *The Guitarist* was an early example of Analytical Cubism.

he found it incompatible with the structure, according to later writings by Kahnweiler. Braque too was more concerned about space than color, saying, "Colour only played a small part. . . . Light was the only aspect of colour that preoccupied us."[16]

Early in the Analytic phase, Picasso completed several portraits. Dissecting a face into cubes and facets was especially startling to observers, but, strangely, Picasso's Cubist faces were usually recognizable, a measure of the artist's genius in this groundbreaking technique. His *Portrait of Daniel-Henri Kahnweiler* (1910) is considered one of the best examples of Analytic Cubism. Picasso also created Cubist portraits of the art dealers Wilhelm Uhde and Ambroise Vollard.

Ordinary Objects

Braque turned to still lifes more than portraits to experiment with perspective and to study composition and the solidity of objects. Both Braque and Picasso preferred to use humble objects in their compositions because they thought these better represented everyday reality. Picasso described the kinds of items he preferred in his paintings as "common objects from anywhere: a pitcher, a mug of beer, a pipe, a package of tobacco, a bowl, a kitchen chair with a cane seat, a plain common table—the object at its most ordinary."[17] Cézanne had also preferred humble domestic objects such as fruits and vegetables, utensils, and stoneware pottery in his still-life compositions, and the two Cubist artists looked again to his work, this time for clues on how to select and arrange such objects for a still-life painting. Braque and Picasso also adapted Cézanne's use of

Braque's painting *Homage to J.S. Bach* reflects the artist's interest in incorporating musical themes into his work.

distorted perspectives and a shifting relationship among objects and the space surrounding them. In addition, they experimented with painting the background first, rather than the foreground, which was the custom of painters at the time.

A talented musician, Braque was the first to use musical instruments in Cubist still lifes, beginning with *Still Life with Musical Instruments*, painted in the autumn of 1908. Music became a favorite theme for Braque, and he often incorporated items such as a metronome, violin, guitar, mandolin, clarinet, or piece of sheet music into his paintings. A 1912 work titled *Homage to J.S. Bach*, for example, depicted a violin on a wooden table with—a revolutionary idea at the time—the superimposed letters of Bach's name seeming to float unattached. In *Violin and Palette* (1909), the forms of a violin and an artist's palette are displayed as though the viewer were looking at them from many different perspectives at once. The result is that the forms seem to melt into one another, which discourages the eye from resting on any one part of the canvas.

Though the two Montmartre artists rarely discussed their art publicly, descriptions of their work spread, and other artists began experimenting with Cubist techniques. A few writers and critics also intrigued by the new art movement formed an informal group known as the *bande à Picasso*, which provided support and encouragement in the early years of Cubism. Members included the writers Apollinaire, Salmon, and Max Jacob. Braque and Picasso remained, however, each other's strongest supporters and collaborators.

The Closest Collaboration

In July 1911 Picasso went to Ceret in the south of France, and Braque joined him there in mid-August. During the next three weeks, the two worked so closely together that their works from this period are almost impossible to tell apart. In fact, some works were such close collaborations that neither artist would sign them as his own. Of this time, Braque later said: "Things were said between us in those years that no one will say again, that no one would know how to say, that no one would understand now."[18]

Creative tension between the two was at its height, and many critics believe their Cubist genius peaked that summer. Braque kept *Still Life with Violin*, which he painted at Ceret that year, all his life to remind him of this intensely creative time.

Two articles published that August and September increased the general public's interest in this new kind of art. The first was an essay titled "Picasso and Braque," which appeared in the August 24 issue of the Italian art-literary magazine *La Voce*. Written by the Florentine painter, critic, and poet Ardengo Soffici, who had befriended the artists while living in Paris from 1900 to 1907, the essay was the first to discuss Picasso and Braque together. The next month, on September 30, an article titled "The Cubists" was published in the Belgian art review *Journal de Bruxelles*. This article proclaimed the "current master" to be Picasso and reported, "As cut up and tottering as his 'cubes' appear, they remain bound together by the old equilibrium,"[19] an indication he was achieving the classical solidity Cézanne had attempted.

Taking Notice of Cubism

The attention was not necessarily welcomed by Braque, who preferred to concentrate on his work. In October he wrote to Kahnweiler: "Every day I have to fight against the people of Ceret who want to see cubism."[20] In fact, it was inevitable that fellow artists working in Montmartre had noticed the Cubist experiments. One in particular, Juan Gris, a young illustrator from Madrid, had a unique vantage point from which to observe and absorb Picasso's work after he moved into an adjacent studio in the ramshackle Bateau-Lavoir in 1906. Gris (born Jose Victoriano Gonzalez) worked as a graphic designer, cartoonist, and magazine illustrator. Though he was not a painter, he was accepted into Picasso's circle and soon became friends with Braque and Matisse as well.

The talented Gris, who began painting in 1910, would make important contributions to Cubism. His public debut in

Henri Matisse worked as a law clerk until 1891, when he began to study art under a conservative painter at an art academy. Matisse, the founder of the Fauves, tried the Cubist approach, muting his palette and making shapes more geometric in works such as The Moroccans *and* The Piano Lesson. *In his view, Braque created the first Cubist works. Matisse later recalled:*

*A*ccording to my recollection, it was Braque who made the first Cubist painting. He brought back from the south a Mediterranean landscape that represented a seaside village seen from above. . . . This is really the first picture constituting the origin of Cubism, and we considered it as something quite new about which there were many discussions.

Pictured in 1951, Matisse works in bed with his cat lounging nearby.

Quoted in William Rubin, *Picasso and Braque: Pioneering Cubism.* New York: Metropolitan Museum of Art, 1989, p. 355.

January 1912 included fifteen paintings shown in a shop next door to the dealer Sagot, who bought a group of his paintings. That spring Gris exhibited three canvases at the 1912 Salon des Indépendants, including the *Portrait of Pablo Picasso*—a work that was called "startlingly accomplished"[21] by contemporary critic David Cottington and is considered a significant early Cubist painting.

Gris too was inspired by Cézanne, which in his case meant experimental use of light and color. This gave his Cubist paintings a more defined and richly colored appearance than those of Braque or Picasso. He developed his own idiom, or means of expression, which included applying sand and ash to a canvas in addition to paint to create textural contrasts.

Besides Gris, another follower quickly emerged as an important contributor to the Cubist movement. Fernand Léger had moved to Paris in 1900 to work as an architectural draftsman and a photographic retoucher. In 1903 he briefly studied painting at the École des Beaux-Arts. Like Braque and Picasso, Léger was inspired by Cézanne's geometric compositions, and by 1910 he had become friendly with both and begun using Cubist techniques in his own work. Léger's approach was distinctive, however: He often used mechanistic shapes such as pistons and cogs and polished tubes that gave his paintings an industrial, machine-age look. He exhibited five paintings at the Salon des Indépendants in 1911, and his 1912 abstract work *Woman in Blue* is considered a Cubist masterpiece.

In addition to the four leading Cubists, others across Paris began experimenting with the Cubist approach. The Belle Époque was rapidly drawing to a close, however. The flourishing of the arts and culture in Europe would last only until 1914, when world war devastated the continent. Cubism's development would be crowded into the brief period from 1909 until the outbreak of war.

The Salon Cubists

After an incubation period in Montmartre, Cubism spread to artists working in other parts of Paris about 1909. The movement became a rallying point for painters who believed the naturalistic approach to art was outdated. Because many different kinds of artists felt this way, the Cubist movement took many different forms in this next phase.

The artists who followed Picasso and Braque became known as Salon Cubists because they exhibited their work primarily in the salons (Braque and Picasso are referred to as Gallery Cubists because they exhibited almost exclusively in private galleries). Many critics consider the Salon Cubists' work to be inferior to that of Braque and Picasso, but other critics argue that it was simply different, and significant in its own way.

In addition to the group of Cubist artists living in Montmartre, two other fairly distinct Cubist groups emerged in Paris. One circle of artists lived on the Left Bank and another lived and worked in the northwest suburbs of Paris.

Cubism's Public Debut

Although Paris's artistic community had been introduced to Cubism in 1908, the general public was not exposed to the genre until 1910, at the spring Salon des Indépendants XXVI and at the Salon d'Automne VIII. Artists who exhibited Cubist works at both salons included Albert Gleizes, Léger, Robert Delaunay, Henri Le Fauconnier, and Jean Metzinger. The first reference to a school of Cubist painters also occurred in the French press that year.

If the juries and public scorned the Impressionists and ridiculed the Fauves, their reaction to the Cubists was outright hostility. They were scandalized by the Cubist paintings, which they thought looked like jumbles of random pieces. An art critic for the French news agency La Presse dubbed the Cubist works at the 1910 salons "geometric follies."[22] One young critic,

Seen in this 1900 photo, the Pont des Arts pedestrian bridge crosses to the Left Bank of the Seine River, where many artists lived.

652

PARIS. — Le Pont des Arts et l'Institut   X. Phot.

however, Roger Allard, singled out for praise works by Gleizes, Le Fauconnier, and Metzinger.

A Room of Their Own

Five of the Salon Cubist painters—Gleizes, Le Fauconnier, Metzinger, Léger, and Delaunay—decided they wanted to exhibit their work as a group at the Salon des Indépendants in April 1911. Having their own exhibit within the overall exhibition required changing two fairly significant salon policies. First, entries normally were exhibited in alphabetical order, but the Cubists wanted to be grouped together. Second, they wanted a room allocated solely to Cubism, another unprecedented request. With the support of critics Apollinaire and Allard, they lobbied the salon officials, who eventually consented to both requests.

The Cubist artists were assigned to Room 41 for the spring salon. The artists who were experienced salon exhibitors knew that the larger their work was, the more attention it attracted. Consequently, each of the five men submitted his largest painting to date. When the Salon des Indépendants opened on April 21, the Cubist room did indeed attract a great deal of attention, though the vast majority of it was negative.

Room 41 featured works by painters besides Delaunay, Gleizes, Le Fauconnier, Léger, and Metzinger. These included Roger de la Fresnaye and Marie Laurencin, one of the few female artists to exhibit with the Cubists, who showed two paintings. Laurencin's interest in Cubism stemmed from a romantic relationship with Apollinaire, who had been introduced to her by Picasso.

Le Fauconnier's *Abundance* immediately emerged as the most famous of the paintings exhibited in Room 41. For his subject matter, Le Fauconnier returned to a more classical motif—that of a mother and child juxtaposed with fruits of nature—but it was rendered through dozens of conflicting panels and confusing pieces, like a puzzle that did not fit together quite right.

Le Fauconnier and other Cubists again exhibited as a group at the autumn salon of 1911. Their persistence and

In 1911, when Salon Cubist painters staged a group exhibit at the Salon des Indépendants, Henri Le Fauconnier's painting *Abundance* stole the show.

growing strength was noted in an article on the exhibition opening published in *Paris-Journal* on September 30. In it, André Salmon wrote: "The Cubists, once isolated skirmishers, engaged in their first pitched battle today."[23]

Apollinaire was critical of the overall quality of the works in the autumn exhibition, and lamented the absence of Picasso. He wrote: "It is a pale imitation, without vigour, of works not shown, painted by an artist endowed with a strong personality and who furthermore has not revealed his secrets to anyone. This great artist is named Pablo Picasso. But the cubism of the Salon d'Automne is a jay dressed up as a peacock."[24]

Since Braque and Picasso steadfastly refused to enter the salons, many of the Salon Cubists had never met either artist. Metzinger and Gris were among the few who knew both men personally and were able to maintain a foot in both the Gallery and Salon Cubist camps. Born in 1883 in Nantes, France, Metzinger had arrived in Paris in 1902, settling in Montmartre, where he undertook a rapid apprenticeship in painting. He met the writer Max Jacob, who introduced him to Apollinaire and his circle, including Braque and Picasso. Another of his early friends in Paris was Delaunay, who introduced him to Le Fauconnier, Gleizes, and Léger. Metzinger's work at the 1909 Salon des Indépendants was singled out by the critic Vauxcelles, who wrote: "He is galloping along behind Picasso or [Fauvist André] Derain or Braque."[25] By the fall of 1911 Metzinger was acknowledged as the Salon Cubists' leading figure, supplanting Le Fauconnier in that role.

The Scandal of 1912

By that time, Cubism was notorious enough to be the subject of widespread debate. The animosity toward the Cubists deepened prior to the 1912 Salon d'Automne, fueled by the president of the salon, who was exceptionally conservative and traditional. The president's anti-Cubist attitude caused Jacques Villon, who had helped organize the drawing section of the first Salon d'Automne in 1903, to resign from the salon committee. The controversy even led to an outburst about the

Cubists in the French Chamber of Deputies. Opposition to the Cubists was so strong that some government officials advocated that their works be banned from public buildings (the autumn salon was held in Paris's great glass-and-steel exhibition hall, the Grand Palais). Eventually, however, the Cubists were allowed to exhibit in the fall 1912 salon.

After the salon opened in October, Apollinaire wrote that the Cubists were not only being mocked as they were the year before, but that "now they were arousing hatred."[26] Picasso and Braque remained apart from the Salon Cubists and were not criticized, even though their work was even more revolutionary than that on public exhibit at the salons.

The hostility toward the Cubist works at the autumn salon was so strong that it prompted one town councilman to write an open letter to the undersecretary in the Ministry of the Arts. A local newspaper published the letter, which read in part: "I hope you will leave feeling as nauseated as many people I know."[27]

The Puteaux Group

Another Cubist exhibition in the fall of 1912 intensified the public debate. It was called the Salon de la Section d'Or (Salon of the Golden Section) and organized by the group of Cubists who gathered regularly at the studio of Jacques Villon on the western outskirts of the Paris suburbs in the village of Puteaux. The group had a common interest in geometry—Villon in particular had long been preoccupied with applying mathematical principles to art—and collectively became known as the Puteaux Group.

Many in the Puteaux Group had gained prominence after exhibiting in Room 41 at the Salon des Indépendants in 1910 and 1911. In addition to Villon and his brothers, Marcel Duchamp and Raymond Duchamp-Villon, artist members of the group included Delaunay, La Fresnaye, Gleizes, Le Fauconnier, Léger, and Metzinger. Gris, who had studied engineering, was a frequent visitor as well, attracted by the group's intellectual and mathematical approach to art.

THE ARTISTIC DUCHAMP FAMILY

The artistic household of Eugène and Lucie Duchamp produced four accomplished Cubist artists among their six children. The children received art lessons from their maternal grandfather, Émile Nicolle. The oldest child, Gaston (who later changed his name to Jacques Villon) was born in 1875. He loved math and studied law but turned to art, becoming a painter and printmaker. Raymond (who adopted the last name Duchamp-Villon) was born in 1876 and became a sculptor, painter, and author. Villon and Duchamp-Villon moved to the Montmartre quarter of Paris in 1894, then to Puteaux in 1906.

Their younger brother Marcel Duchamp, born in 1887, trained as a librarian and then as an illustrator and inventor. He was not only an influential Cubist but an important member of the later Surrealist and Dadaist movements as well. Suzanne Duchamp, born in 1889, began to study art at the École des Beaux-Arts when she was sixteen. At the age of twenty-two she had her first major exhibit at the Salon des Indépendants. She was an Impressionist and Cubist before evolving into a Dadaist when that movement emerged after the end of World War I.

The core of the group were the three brothers. The oldest, christened Gaston Émile Duchamp in 1875, was the first of six children born to an artistic family that produced four famous artists (three sons and a daughter), all involved at some point with the Cubist movement. He later adopted a pseudonym so he would not be confused with his artist siblings, choosing the name Jacques Villon as a tribute to the French medieval poet François Villon.

Villon and his brother Raymond moved to Paris in 1894. Villon intended to study law but sought and got his father's permission to study art, soon losing interest in law entirely. He worked as an illustrator for ten years before moving to the quieter area of Puteaux in 1906. Though strongly drawn to Cubism, his isolation from the Montmartre art community and his introverted nature meant that his early efforts went unnoticed.

That changed with the establishment of the Puteaux Group. When these artists met on Sunday afternoons at Villon's studio, they read and discussed works by Leonardo da Vinci and others who wrote about classical mathematics and art. By applying formal rules of geometry and proportion to create form and order, the Puteaux Group refined Cubism's intellectual approach. Villon applied Cubism's analytic theories to volume and linear perspective, and the group was also preoccupied with how movement could be depicted in two-dimensional art.

The artists tackled another challenge as well. In his recently published theory of relativity, Albert Einstein had added to the traditional three dimensions of space—height, width, and depth—a fourth dimension: time. Apollinaire chronicled the Puteaux Group's attempt to conquer this elusive fourth dimension in his book *Les Peintres Cubistes (The Cubist Painters):*

> Until now, the three dimensions of Euclidian geometry were enough to answer the disquiet that a sense of infinity instills in the soul of great artists. The new painters do not claim to be geometricians any more than painters of the past did. But it is true that geometry is to the plastic arts what grammar is to the art of the writer. Nowadays, scientists have gone beyond the three dimensions of Euclidian geometry. Painters have been led, quite naturally and one might say intuitively, to take an interest in the new possibilities for measuring space which in the modern artist's studio were simply and collectively referred to as the *fourth dimension.*[28]

The Section d'Or

The Puteaux Group's mathematics-based discussions carried the concept of art based on intellectualism, rather than emotion,

A drawing by iconic fifteenth-century artist Leonardo da Vinci shows his careful attention to proportion and geometry, elements that the Puteaux Cubists emphasized.

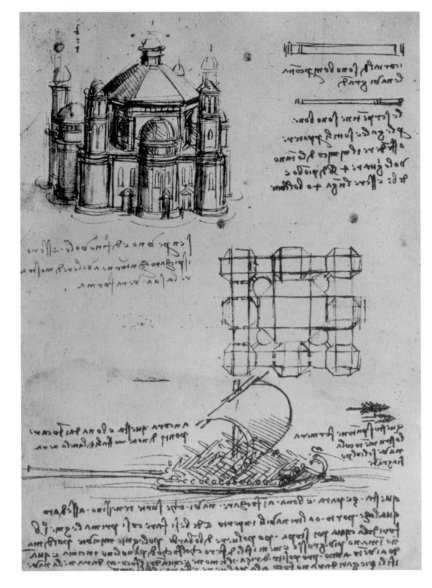

to the extreme. The group believed that reality was best revealed through symbolic geometries, the most famous of which was the golden section ratio, which they experimented with in their works. A theory of proportion developed by the ancient Greek mathematician Euclid, in simplified terms the golden section ratio is the most pleasing, or perfect, relationship of a whole to its parts. Euclid calculated this ratio as 1.62 to 1. That is, the most harmoniously sized rectangle has a height-to-width ratio of 1.62:1; likewise, the ideal ratio of the well-proportioned human body's height to arm span, the parts of a building's decorative facade, and a single line segment divided into two parts is always 1.62:1, the so-called golden ratio.

Villon was so taken with this concept of form and artistic proportion that in 1912 he suggested the group name itself the Section d'Or (Section of Gold, or Golden Section). His motto for creating order in paintings was: "Where cubism uproots, the Section d' Or implants. While the first is rethinking perspective, the other wants to penetrate its secrets."[29] Although the name was Villon's brainchild, it was his younger brother, Marcel Duchamp, who conceived the idea of an independent Section d'Or exhibition.

The inaugural Salon de la Section d'Or was timed to coincide with the traditional autumn salon. The Section d'Or Salon opened on October 10, 1912, in the Galerie La Boétie in Paris, with thirty-one artists showing about two hundred works. Though many of the works did not adhere to the golden section law of proportion, the concentration of influential artists was impressive. Essays by nineteen writers were included in *La Section d'Or*, a collection of articles published to accompany the exhibition. One of the articles proclaimed: "For the first time, such a complete grouping of all the artists who have inaugurated the 20th century with works clearly representative of the tastes, the tendencies and the ideas which characterise it."[30] Again, however, Braque and Picasso were notably absent.

The most talked-about artists at the Section d'Or exhibition were Gris and Duchamp. Gris exhibited the humorous *Man in a Café*, which managed to portray the impatient movement of a top-hatted sophisticate. The writer Maurice Raynal found Gris to be the "fiercest of the purists" in the Section d'Or salon.

> We never, in fact, see an object in all its dimensions at once. Therefore what has to be done is to fill in the gap in our seeing. Conception gives us the means. Conception makes us aware of the objects that we would not be able to see . . . and so, if the painter succeeds in

rendering the object in all its dimensions, he achieves a work of method which is of a higher order than one painted according to the visual dimension only.[31]

In the Section d'Or show Duchamp was at last able to show his *Nude Descending a Staircase*, which had been rejected by the Salon des Indépendants earlier in the year. Duchamp's painting was considered revolutionary because of the flurry of movement it depicted. To indicate action, Duchamp used a series of overlapping shapes that made a figure seem to be moving down the stairs, in much the way a multiple-exposure photograph shows the sequence of movements of a single person. Though the painting outraged many viewers and confused others—affirming their idea that modern art was unintelligible —the painting caused a sensation both at the Paris show and the next year, when it was exhibited at the U.S. Armory Show in New York City, the first large-scale display of modern art in the United States.

Marcel Duchamp exhibited his *Nude Descending a Staircase* at the Salon de la Section d'Or.

The Cubist House

The Section d'Or group undertook another ambitious project in 1912. Known as the Cubist House, the project was conceived by the interior decorator André Mare and Duchamp-Villon, who was a sculptor. It consisted of a suite of furnished interiors assembled for the 1912 Salon d'Automne. Orchestrated by Mare, the Cubist House involved most of the members of the Puteaux circle. The artists wanted to apply Cubist principles to decorative arts and used simple lines and bright colors to design the rooms' interiors and furnishings. Cubist paintings hung on the walls. Visitors entered the suite of rooms, which included an entrance porch, hall, living room and bedroom, through a plaster facade built by Duchamp-Villon, which served as the entrance. It opened onto three colorful and fully furnished rooms with wood paneling, a fireplace, specially made furniture, rugs, lights, pictures, ornaments, and art objects including a clock made by La Fresnaye.

The Cubist House was much talked about by visitors to the 1912 fall salon and earned the Cubists even more notoriety. The publicity, as usual, was negative. Two weeks after the Cubist House debuted, Allard dryly noted that the "Cubist House had already received more insults than a Cubist painting."[32]

Allard and other writers familiar with the Cubists' work were instrumental in their rising reputation, both positive and negative. In addition, the artists Metzinger and Gleizes published articles and a book about the movement. Metzinger had several articles on contemporary art published and was the first to note in print that Picasso and Braque had dismissed traditional perspective and merged multiple viewpoints in a single image. Metzinger and Gleizes published the first book on the subject, *Du Cubisme* (*On Cubism*), in November 1912. Apollinaire began his book about Cubism in 1912, and it was published the next spring as *Les Peintres Cubistes* (*The Cubist Painters*) with the subtitle *Aesthetic Meditations*.

A multiple exposure photo of Marcel Duchamp evokes his *Staircase* painting.

Reflecting Modern Society

By the time Apollinaire's book was published, the Cubists had moved beyond familiar domestic items, such as fruit and stoneware, in their paintings. They were now more interested in objects that reflected an urban setting and modern times: a café table, playing cards, cigars, pipes, newspapers, bottles. Cubist artists found many possibilities in these simple objects, which appeared over and over again in their work. Delaunay's favorite subjects were miracles of modern engineering, such as the Eiffel Tower, airplanes, and the Ferris wheel.

Delaunay and his wife, Sonia, were among the first Cubists to find inspiration in the urban landscape. A native of Paris, he loved the color, rhythm, and energy of the city. Without any formal art training, he started as an Impressionist painter and then experimented with Fauvism before being introduced to Cubism through Metzinger and Apollinaire. By 1909 his own work involved the application of color to Cubist principles. His series of thirty paintings of the Eiffel Tower, begun in 1910, established him as a Cubist artist.

Delaunay's *Homage to Bleriot* was a tribute to Louis Bleriot, who in 1909 became the first person to fly across the English Channel. His painting *The Rugby Team*, painted in 1912–1913, was full of symbols of modern life—sports, an airplane, the Eiffel Tower, and a Ferris wheel. *The Cardiff Team* took its subject from a newspaper photo of a rugby match and incorporated imagery from billboards. His painting *Political Drama* was drawn from a real-life scandal involving the editor of a leading conservative newspaper, who was shot by the wife of the French finance minister. Several of Delaunay's paintings, including one of the Eiffel Tower, appeared to be urban scenes glimpsed through a window, and he used the window metaphor in a dozen paintings in the summer of 1912.

Like her husband, Sonia Delaunay, a Russian native who immigrated to Paris in 1905, was also fascinated by urban scenes and new technologies, such as the automobile and cinema. Her painting *Electric Prisms* celebrated aviation and electric lighting. Both Delaunays preferred vivid colors, and their contrasting use of warm and cool colors in circular patterns distinguished their work from that of the other Cubists. They believed the vivid colors best captured the movement and dynamic vision of a modern city.

Guillaume Apollinaire: Promoter of Cubism

Guillaume Apollinaire was born in Rome in 1880 to an Italian father and a Polish mother. He was educated in France and made his home in the Montmartre district of Paris, where he got to know Picasso and other artists. He was one of the first to appreciate the work of Matisse, Braque, and Picasso, and he published a book and many articles on Cubism.

In addition to being an important chronicler of the Cubist movement, Apollinaire was France's foremost poet. In both roles, he exalted the new and exciting, which included Cubism. In 1911 he explained the new style of art: "Cubism is not, as the public generally thinks, the art of painting everything in the form of cubes. In 1908 we saw several paintings by Picasso depicting some simply and solidly drawn houses, which gave to the public the illusion of such cubes, and thus the name of our youngest school of painting was born."

Though Apollinaire was not required to enlist because he was born in Italy, he joined the French military when World War I broke out in 1914. He received a head wound in 1916 and, his health compromised, died in 1918 from Spanish influenza.

An artist depicts Guillaume Apollinaire (right) and his friend, poet Max Jacob, in a Parisian café.

Quoted in William Rubin, *Picasso and Braque: Pioneering Cubism.* New York: Metropolitan Museum of Art, 1989, p. 381.

Branches of Cubism

The Delaunays were responsible for the branch of Cubism known as Orphism, or Orphic Cubism. In 1912 Apollinaire applied the French term *Orphisme* to their colorful interpretation of Cubism, which he saw as visionary and lyrical. The reference is to Orpheus, a poet and musician in Greek mythology. Apollinaire wrote: "Delaunay, on his own, was silently inventing an art of pure colour. Thus we are moving towards an entirely new form of art, which will be to painting . . . what music is to poetry. It will be pure painting."[33] Apollinaire saw the color harmonies in the Delaunays' works as corresponding to musical pitches.

The Delaunays were not the only artists to create new forms of Cubism. Tubism, for example, was an informal term coined to describe works that relied heavily on tubular, machinelike shapes. It is used most often in reference to works by Léger, whose works frequently depicted Paris rooftops and factories.

The interpretations of Cubism developed by Léger and the Delaunays influenced many of the salon artists, who followed their lead in experimenting with brighter colors and mechanical shapes. Yet even as they did, the original founders of Cubism were poised to take the movement in an entirely new direction.

Synthetic Cubism: Moving to Three Dimensions

While the Salon Cubists were bringing the movement its first widespread public attention, its inventors were already in uncharted territory, launching a second phase of Cubism that emerged in 1912. Having pushed the exploration of two-dimensional painting as far as they could, Braque and Picasso again took the lead, this time incorporating paper, typography, and found objects into their works—something that had never been done before. This phase became known as Synthetic Cubism because it synthesized various materials, bringing elements together in new forms instead of fragmenting objects as in Analytic Cubism. The process engendered two new media: collage, from the French word *coller*, meaning to paste or glue; and *papier-collé*, meaning glued papers. Works of collage combine various flat materials into a new whole; *papier-collé* is a form of collage in which the materials pasted to the canvas are in the shapes of recognizable object.

Because Cubism evolved so much in 1912—when Picasso created the first collage and Braque the first *papier-collé*—that year marks the dividing point between the Analytic and Synthetic phases of Cubism. While Analytic Cubism depended on scrutiny of its subject, Synthetic Cubism was not as concerned with exploring the anatomy and structure of nature and objects. The focus instead was on the construction of art rather than the analysis of the subject.

One element of Braque and Picasso's Synthetic Cubism—the addition of words and letters into their artwork—was an outgrowth of techniques the two had already experimented with. Both had painted letters and numerals in various works. For example, Braque had called on his experience as a house painter to incorporate letters and numbers into works such as *Match-box and Newspaper* in 1910. Picasso tried a similar experiment the next year. During the summer of 1911 both used words, letters, and symbols as elements in their paintings, not just as pure images but as words with meaning relevant to the subject. Picasso continued using this technique in the winter of 1911–1912, when he added the words "MA JOLIE" ("my pretty one") at the bottom of a painting titled *Woman with Guitar*. The phrase referred both to his new love interest, Eva Gouel, as well as to the name of a current popular song.

The First Collage

Picasso tried another revolutionary experiment in the spring of 1912. At the time no one thought it possible to create art without oil paint, watercolor, pencils, or charcoal. Earlier in the year Picasso had started to use enamel house paint in place of his usual oils in some pictures. But in May he made an even more radical leap when he glued onto a canvas a fragment of oilcloth with a pre-printed chair-caning pattern. He completed the work—titled *Still Life with Chair Caning*—by edging the canvas with a piece of real rope. By introducing an actual item into a painted representation of reality, he created another way to imitate reality, and unwittingly invented the technique of collage.

Picasso did not return to the art form, however, until after Braque completed the first *papier-collé* that fall. Braque and Picasso spent the summer of 1912 at Sorgues, a village north of Avignon. By the time Picasso returned to Paris in September, the two had realized they could carry their analytical methods no further. While Picasso was in Paris, Braque bought a reproduction of oak paneling in a shop in Avignon. The simulated wood was similar to the effect he had been creating by running a metal comb through his paint.

Braque used the oak-grained paper to represent a paneled background and a wood table. He wrote the word BAR at the top and ALE at the bottom, and the result, *Fruit Dish and Glass*, became the first *papier-collé*. Pierre Daix, a leading Cubist critic, described the innovation: "Never before had the painter so completely destroyed the mystery of his work, never before did he present himself to the scrutiny of the spectator, not only without the tricks of the trade, but using means that are within

In creating the first collage, *Still Life with Chair Caning*, Picasso employed radically new artistic techniques.

Like his first *papier-collé,* Braque's 1912 work titled *Papier Collé* incorporates oak-grained paper, along with other paper elements.

everyone's grasp. And never before had a painter asserted his power as a creator, as a poet in the strongest sense of the word."[34]

Braque created an impressive series of *papier-collé* works that fall. He experimented with gluing overlapping and fragmented pieces of newspaper, wallpaper, tickets, cigarette packages, and other paper objects. He eventually made a total of sixty-five *papiers-collé* works but apparently did not take this new art form seriously because few of these have survived. Others, however, were impressed with the innovative techniques of incorporating papers, textures, and words into drawings and paintings. Pierre Cabanne, a prominent French critic and author of the book *Cubism*, singled Braque out for praise, writing that he was "the true initiator of this revolution. Several months will go by before the Spaniard [Picasso] is able to catch up with him."[35]

For his part, Picasso became so obsessed with these new techniques that he abandoned painting almost entirely for several months during the autumn of 1912. *Glass and Bottle of Suze* is one of his first *papiers-collé*, and one of a series that used little more than pieces of newspaper and charcoal drawings. His *Bottle and Wine Glass on a Table* of 1912 is an early example of Synthetic Cubism that used pasted newsprint and colored paper. In his *Siphon, Glass, Newspaper, and Violin*, also completed in 1912, the cut-out word "JOURNAL" represented a newspaper on a table.

Free from Constraints

Braque and Picasso found that the playful use of words and pasted papers added a whole new dimension to their art, allowing them to use humor or to raise serious questions. At the time newspapers were full of news about the Balkans and the threat of war with Germany. A close reading of the fine print text used in their works of this period revealed not only this kind of news, but news of other events as well: murders, suicides, burglaries, romance, scandal. The artists found that using text from newspapers or books gave viewers an added jolt of reality when they realized the words were about contemporary events. Picasso also simply liked to disorient viewers by placing objects from the real world into the illusory world of art.

Sometimes Picasso used marbled or patterned paper to represent tabletops or walls. Objects drawn over collaged elements produced a different shift in perception and multiple viewpoints, in keeping with the trademark technique of the Cubists. He found almost limitless possibilities with the devices of lettering, collage, and pasted papers, and combined all of these elements in *Violin, Bottle, and Glass* in 1913.

Another hallmark of the second phase for Braque and Picasso was that they began to add more color into their works. They seemed finally free from the somber palette constraints they had imposed on themselves in the Analytic phase while they focused on form and structure. Bright colors and decorative patterns replaced the muted palettes of Cubism's earlier years. Picasso's forms also became larger and more representational during the Synthetic phase.

In 1913, fascinated by the possibilities of this new direction, Braque and Picasso synthesized all kinds of material into their works: found objects, wallpaper, newspapers, playing cards, cigarette wrappers, ornamental patterns, even a real calling card.

PICASSO'S SYNTHETIC CUBIST ASSEMBLAGES

The French artist André Breton recalled what it was like to see photographs of Picasso's Synthetic Cubist assemblages when they were published in a French journal in 1913:

Four of them were composed of an assemblage of materials of a residual nature such as slats, spools, discarded fragments of linoleum, lengths of string, all borrowed from everyday life. The initial shock provoked by an entirely new visual experience was succeeded by an awareness of the incomparable balance achieved by these works, which were thus endowed, willy-nilly, with an organic life that justified the necessity of their existence. Since then nearly half a century has gone by . . . but the image that remains of them suffices to demonstrate to what degree they anticipate those forms of expression today which are most convinced of their own daring.

Quoted in Douglas Cooper and Gary Tinterow, *The Essential Cubism 1907–1920*. London: Tate Gallery, 1983, p. 364.

Gris, who had quickly absorbed Cubist lessons, took to collage as well. In 1913 he too converted to Synthetic Cubism and began making extensive use of *papier-collé* and then collage in works such as *Glasses, Newspaper and a Bottle of Wine*. He also experimented with combining collage and sculpture by adding to his work three-dimensional objects such as wood and nails.

That year Picasso also created several assemblages using items such as wood, cardboard, string, and wallpaper. He also made several constructions out of painted wood. One of his early assemblages was *Guitar Player*, which consisted of a real guitar and two arms made of newspaper to represent the player.

Cubist Sculptures

The next logical step was applying Cubist techniques to sculpture. Though the movement is usually associated with painting, Cubism also had a significant influence on twentieth-century sculpture and architecture. An extremely prolific artist who produced twenty thousand pieces in his lifetime, Picasso created a considerable number of sculptures. Braque, by contrast, produced relatively few, but each one was important.

Braque's interest in sculpture began in August 1911, when he created a relief construction that essentially was a three-dimensional work of *papier-collé* or collage. Braque did not think of this work as a sculpture, however. Picasso had already experimented with sculpture prior to his Cubist period, and returned to the medium in 1912 with *Guitar*, which is considered by some critics to be the first Cubist sculpture. Made of cardboard, pasted paper, string, and canvas, *Guitar* explored the relationship between mass and volume.

Picasso did not use durable materials in his sculptures until 1913. His sculpture *Glass of Absinthe*, completed in the spring of 1914, used a real silver-plated sugar strainer in the wax model. Kahnweiler had six bronze casts made, and Picasso painted each one differently.

A few other artists of the period accomplished significant strides in translating the Cubist idiom into solid sculptural

In Picasso's early sculpture *Glass of Absinthe,* the innovative artist presents both the glass and its contents, piled atop one another and crowned with a sugar lump.

form. These included the French artists Henri Laurens and Raymond Duchamp-Villon as well as Jacques Lipchitz, a native of Lithuania, and the Ukrainian Alexander Archipenko. Laurens had been a friend of Braque's since 1911. "Among the sculptors of cubism [Laurens] is the closest to the painters,"[36] writes art historian Pierre Cabanne. Laurens began to adopt his friend's structural techniques in his works, experimenting with *papier-collé* and then sculpture. *The Spanish Dancer*, a painted-wood sculpture completed in 1914–1915, was among his first three-dimensional Cubist works. In 1915 he created *The Clown*, a painted-wood three-dimensional work that explored different combinations of form and space.

Lipchitz had lived in Paris since October 1909, when he was eighteen. He studied at the École des Beaux-Arts and lived in the Montparnasse district, where he met Diego Rivera, a Mexican painter on the fringes of the Cubism movement. Rivera introduced Lipchitz to Picasso and other artists, and he later formed a close friendship with Gris. Lipchitz made his first sculptures in 1913–1914, and *Head*, completed in 1915, was his first Cubist-inspired sculpture. He modeled his Cubist sculptures first in plaster, and then a professional stone carver reproduced the plaster original in stone. Bronze casts were made of some of the sculptures, including *Sailor with Guitar* (1914).

Duchamp-Villon, a member of the Puteaux circle, had long been an advocate of sculpture and Cubism. He had participated on the jury selecting sculpture for the Salon d'Automne in 1907. Duchamp-Villon was working on preliminary models of what would become his most famous work, a geometrically faceted sculpture titled *The Horse*, when war broke out in Europe and he was called to military service. He managed to complete a final plaster version of the sculpture, ingeniously combining a horse's physiognomy and machinery, on leave in the fall of 1914.

War Changes Everything

Life in Paris was changed drastically when France went to war against Germany in 1914. The Great War, as World War I was called, destroyed traditional European society and had a profound effect on the Cubist movement, which would never regain the momentum it had in the prewar years. The dialogue between the two great artists who had founded Cubism was silenced on August 2, 1914, when Picasso took Braque to the train station and Braque left to join the French 223rd Infantry.

In addition to Duchamp-Villon and Braque, several other important Cubists were sent to the front lines. Gleizes, La Fresnaye, Léger, and Metzinger were among the artists who served in the French army. The remaining Cubists and their circle scattered: The Delaunays sat out the war in Spain;

Marcel Duchamp left for New York; Laurencin had married a German and so went into in exile in Spain; Kahnweiler went into exile in Switzerland. Though Apollinaire had been born in Rome and was not required to enlist, he volunteered to join the French forces. "The old life was over,"[37] wrote Gertrude Stein, who sold pieces of her art collection to finance her supply-delivery efforts during the war.

As Spaniards, Gris and Picasso were not required to join the French army, but the war affected them nonetheless. When Kahnweiler left Paris in mid-1914 for his annual holiday, he took no precautions to protect his gallery's large stock of paintings, even though war seemed imminent. Within months, all German nationals living in France were declared enemy aliens by the government, and his inventory of paintings was confiscated. He not only lost his gallery and paintings but was also prohibited from returning to France for the duration of the war. The same thing happened to the art collector Uhde, who was also German. The artists who remained in Paris, including Gris and Picasso, found they no longer had a gallery or income, and that there were no buyers for their paintings. When Gris, who was under contract to Kahnweiler, attempted to secure his own buyers, however, the art dealer mustered the bravado to threaten to sue him when he returned to France.

The Toll of War

Picasso did not suffer financially during the war, because he had made a good deal of money in the prewar years. This success had allowed him to move from quarters in Montmartre to more spacious lodging—with a maidservant—in the upscale Montparnasse neighborhood, where he moved in higher society than his artist friends. However, he was lonely and unhappy in early wartime Paris. His lover, Eva, was dying of tuberculosis, and he grew increasingly despondent. Stein, however, believed that during the war years of 1914 to 1917 Picasso reached the peak of his Cubist period, "when his mastery of technique became so complete that it reached perfection, there was no longer any hesitation."[38]

The war took a terrible toll on many of the other Cubists and their associates, however. Duchamp-Villon and Apollinaire both died in 1918. Only forty-two years old, Duchamp-Villon died on October 9 as a result of the typhoid fever he had contracted in 1916 while serving in a military hospital at Champagne. His masterpiece, *The Horse*, was cast in bronze after his death. Apollinaire died on November 9 as a result of war injuries and complications from the Spanish flu pandemic. La Fresnaye's health was ruined by his service and he died in 1925 at the age of forty.

DANIEL-HENRI KAHNWEILER, INFLUENTIAL ART DEALER

Daniel-Henri Kahnweiler was instrumental in promoting Cubist art. He was born in 1884 in the Jewish community of Mannheim in Germany and moved to Paris in 1902. He trained to be a banker or stock-broker, but his real interest was art, and he opened a small gallery in Paris in 1907. Kahnweiler signed Picasso and Braque to exclusive contracts in 1912, and then later added Léger and Gris. The art dealer's connections secured important avant-garde exhibitions abroad for his artists.

When World War I broke out, Kahnweiler took refuge in neutral Switzerland. Even though the war had seemed inevitable, he had not taken any precautions to protect his inventory of art, and it was impounded and later auctioned by the French government. While in exile, Kahnweiler wrote *Der Weg zum Kubismus (The Rise of Cubism)*, an important article in support of Cubism. He did not return to Paris until 1920, when he opened a new gallery and renewed contracts with Braque, Léger, and Gris.

When the Germans occupied Paris during World War II, Kahnweiler was again forced to flee. He survived the war, returned to Paris, and opened yet another gallery.

Fernand Léger's noted postwar painting *Soldiers Playing at Cards* showcased the mechanical style called Tubism.

Léger nearly died in the war as the result of a mustard gas attack, but he survived and after the war resumed his work in the mechanical style known as Tubism. Some critics speculated that Léger's art actually improved because of his war assignment as a stretcher carrier, which put him face-to-face with the full horror of war along the front lines. Léger's postwar paintings most often dealt with death, courage, and technology. One of his best-known works was *Soldiers Playing at Cards*, which he painted in 1917 after several weeks in the hospital recovering from his war wounds. The painting depicted robot-like men composed of interlocking geometric shapes. Some critics interpreted his Tubist fragmentation of forms to reflect the world being torn apart by war.

Braque, too, was injured in the war, suffering a serious head wound at Carency in 1915. He began a lengthy convalescence, returning home from the front in March 1916. He experienced severe physical pain from the head injury and suffered a great deal psychologically when he attempted to start painting again. He did not pick up his paintbrushes again until 1917, three years after leaving for military service.

Another casualty of the war was the association between Picasso and Braque. There is no evidence that the two corresponded during the war or that Picasso visited Braque during his long convalescence. Even after Braque recovered, he and Picasso never attempted to reclaim the relationship they had had before the war.

Postwar Paris

Even without Picasso's collaboration, Braque returned to his art when he was finally able to work again. He began with *papier-collé*. His forms were bolder, and he used a wider range of pasted elements. His works from 1917 to 1919 were seen as the culmination of Synthetic Cubism. One of his most ambitious and significant works—in terms of both his lifework and Synthetic Cubism—was *The Musician*, created in 1917–1918. It incorporated rich shades of red, blue, and gray and beautifully elongated patterns.

Though Braque returned to Cubism, his angular forms became more graceful in his postwar work. A decade after his first exhibit at Kahnweiler's gallery in November 1908, he had his second one-man show in March 1919, showing ten still lifes. The exhibition was at a gallery owned by Leonce Rosenberg, who had taken advantage of the dearth of galleries during the war and opened his own. He had signed some of the Cubists to contracts after the war was over, but Kahnweiler reclaimed most of them when he returned to Paris in the second half of 1920 and opened a new gallery.

In 1920 the last Cubist group exhibition was organized for the Salon des Indépendants to show the solidarity of painters whose styles were still under attack by conservative critics. Cubists who exhibited in this salon included the painters Gleizes, Gris, Léger, Metzinger, and Villon, and the sculptors Archipenko and Lipchitz. Braque agreed to be part of the exhibition, and for the first time since 1909 exhibited in a salon. The other great Gallery Cubist—Picasso—again refused to participate. However, Picasso finally did join other Cubists for the third exhibition of the Section d'Or, organized in 1925.

Unlike Braque, who remained fairly true to Cubist standards, Picasso's style took other forms throughout his long career. In the early 1920s Picasso's work became more colorful and he returned to some of the circus figures he had favored during his Rose Period, such as in *Pierrot and Harlequin*, com-

According to some critics, Picasso's 1921 painting *Three Musicians* marked the end of the Cubist era in France.

pleted in 1920. He continued experimenting with Synthetic Cubist techniques, however. *Three Musicians*, painted in the summer of 1921, is seen by some critics as the juncture where Synthetic Cubism and naturalism met.

Though the point at which the Cubist period ended can be debated as heatedly as the point at which it began, many critics view *Three Musicians* as signaling the end of the Cubist era in France. With the loss of some key Cubists and new directions by others, Cubism ceased to exist as a collective movement. Yet it continued to take on different forms and to influence the direction of modern art.

Cubism's Influence: Moving to Total Abstraction

Within four years of its creation in Paris, Cubism had captured the imaginations of artists in Germany, Holland, Italy, Czechoslovakia, Russia, and the United States, as well as France outside of Paris. As Cubism spread the new artistic language was refined and developed new forms of expression. In Czechoslovakia for example, Cubist principles governed the design of apartment buildings and home furnishings.

Although some artists profoundly affected by Cubism remained loyal to the tenets of its inventors, naturally others did not. These artists' interpretations differed so much from that of Braque and Picasso that they eventually founded separate art movements, just as Braque and Picasso credited Cézanne's huge influence but searched for individual artistic vision. Braque and Picasso had chosen not to venture into total abstraction, but their groundbreaking experiments with fragmentation and multiple viewpoints blazed the trail for abstract art around the world. As the first movement to take a significant step away from realism, Cubism formed a vital link between traditional and modern art. Once Cubists rejected convention, artists in France and other countries felt freer to pursue art that was not strictly representational.

Czechoslovakia embraced Cubism, reflected here in a villa designed by Czech architect Josef Chochol in 1913.

Indeed, art had already become increasingly abstract in the prewar years. As the threat of war hung heavily over Europe, artists began to search for ways to better reflect the complex and unsettled world around them. Once war broke out in 1914 and the number of casualties quickly rose, an increasing number of artists broke ties with tradition and pursued more radical approaches that reflected the senselessness around them. Swiss artist Paul Klee expressed the feeling of his generation in 1915: "The more terrifying the world becomes . . . the more art becomes abstract."[39]

Moving Beyond Paris

Sonia and Robert Delaunay were among the first artists to cross the threshold to true abstraction. Paintings they completed in the Orphic Cubism style in 1912–1913 are cited by some historians as being the first abstract paintings. Within a year, three artists who would have a significant impact on the development of abstract art followed suit: Wassily Kandinsky and Kasimir Malevich in Russia and Piet Mondrian in the Netherlands. All three were strongly influenced by Cubism. In addition to a tendency toward abstraction, the movements and styles that grew out of Cubism and were influenced by it shared a preoccupation with contemporary themes, usually urban, or had a geometric component. Though these new approaches took different forms, avant-garde artists of the period were united by a desire to find a satisfactory way to represent the reality of their time.

Artists in other countries had learned about French Cubism through published articles, foreign art collectors, and exhibitions. Though reluctant to do so, Picasso was persuaded by Gertrude Stein to show eighty-three drawings and watercolors at the Alfred Stieglitz Gallery in New York City in 1911. Because of this one-man show Picasso was considered in the United States to be the undisputed creator of Cubism. Braque and Picasso also exhibited in London, Munich, and at the Modern Kunst Kring (Currents in Modern Art exhibition) in Amsterdam.

Mexican Cubism: Diego Rivera

The famous Mexican muralist Diego Rivera went through a Cubist period after becoming friends with Picasso. Rivera first went to Europe to study in 1907 when he was twenty years old. Picasso's influence is particularly evident in several paintings Rivera created between 1913 and 1916. Rivera showed masterful technique in many Cubist portraits as well as still lifes and scenes of Paris, such as one of a café table and one of the Eiffel Tower.

He used transparent planes and everyday objects to communicate themes of identity and place during the years of World War I and the Mexican Revolution. Works such as *Zapatista Landscape* incorporated traditional emblems of Mexican identity, including the colors of the Mexican flag, serapes, and gourds.

On a visit to Italy, Rivera was inspired by the church frescoes there. He saw them as a way poor people could enjoy art, and so returned home to his native country to concentrate on painting murals.

After discovering Cubism at the Modern Kunst Kring in 1911, Mondrian was inspired to visit Paris and start developing Cubist ideas in an abstract way. He spent several years there passionately absorbing the lessons of Cubism. Like the Cubists, he was concerned with how to translate three-dimensional objects onto a two-dimensional plane. Apollinaire noted "Mondrian's very abstract cubism"[40] in the Salon des Indépendants of 1913.

Mondrian's work evolved from abstract Cubism to a distinctive style that was severely geometric: Many canvases consisted of solid blocks of red, blue, and yellow on a white background, separated by heavy black horizontal and vertical lines.

"Little by little I became aware of the fact that cubism didn't accept the logical consequences of my discoveries, it didn't take abstraction to its ultimate goal, the expression of true reality,"[41] he later wrote.

In addition to the artists themselves, art dealers such as Kahnweiler and Uhde were important in spreading awareness of Cubist works. Even though Kahnweiler had a gallery in Paris, his French customers were far outnumbered by art collectors in the United States, Russia, Switzerland, and Austria. The Czech Vincenc Kramar, director of the National Gallery in Prague, also bought many fine Cubist paintings by Braque and Picasso.

Exposure in Germany

As artists outside France began to experiment with Cubism, Robert Delaunay provided a link between French Cubism and the research being done by the Blue Rider group in Munich. This group was formed by Kandinsky and the German artist Franz Marc, who had been drawn to the Delaunays' Orphic Cubism. Delaunay showed his works in Berlin at the Der Sturm Gallery and at the first Blue Rider exhibition in Munich in 1911. Kandinsky had initially been attracted to the Fauves and then to the Cubists as his own style evolved toward abstraction using pure, bright colors.

Toward the end of 1911, Kandinsky met Paul Klee, who had settled in Munich. Klee saw Cubist works in two Blue Rider exhibitions that winter. He was so drawn to the art form that he traveled to Paris in the spring of 1912 to study it further. He visited the Salon des Indépendants as well as Uhde's and Kahnweiler's galleries. At the salon he saw works by Léger, Le Fauconnier, Gris, Duchamp, and La Fresnaye. He was so impressed by Delaunay's large *La Ville de Paris (City of Paris)* and his series of paintings of the Eiffel Tower that he obtained a letter of introduction from Kandinsky so he could meet the artist.

French Cubists who exhibited at the next Blue Rider exhibition included Braque, La Fresnaye, Picasso, and Delaunay. The exhibition provided the most numerous examples of Cubism yet seen in Munich, and it gave Klee plenty to study. Jim Jordan, the author of *Paul Klee and Cubism*, writes: "Over the next several years, Klee showed a progressive understanding and adaptation of these aspects of high Analytical Cubism."[42]

Coming to America

Outside of Europe, a massive art show in 1913 at New York City's 69th Infantry Regiment Armory introduced Americans to Cubism and modern art. The impact of the International Exhibition of Modern Art—known informally as the U.S. Armory Show—on the future direction of art in the United

CUBISM IN WRITING AND MUSIC

The term *Cubism* is sometimes applied to music and literature of the early twentieth century as well as to art. Writers James Joyce and Virginia Woolf (born within a year of Braque and Picasso) introduced fragmented Cubist techniques into their sensational novels *Ulysses* and *Mrs. Dalloway*, respectively. In both of these novels, the narrative sequence is limited to one day, but it is one filled with the complexity of multiple experiences and contradictory interpretations. Gertrude Stein's unique repetitive and sometimes nonsensical writing style has also been called Cubist.

In music, the Cubists' contemporary Igor Stravinsky created a new approach to musical structure that could be called Cubist because he broke its melody into fragmentary and shifting rhythmic patterns. He also experimented with dissonant tones sounded simultaneously.

States cannot be overstated. The exhibition was eye opening not only for the general public but for American artists and critics as well, many of whom had been oblivious to the advances in art being made in Europe. The Armory Show is considered the most significant event in the history of American art, the pivotal moment marking the beginning the modern age. More than seventy thousand spectators visited the exhibition between February 17 and March 15, 1913. For many of them, the show provided their first glimpses of both Fauvism and Cubism.

The exhibition was organized by a fledging group of sixteen progressive American artists called the Association of American Painters and Sculptors, whose representatives toured Europe in the summer of 1912 and selected sixteen hundred works by about three hundred artists to be included in the show. Picasso was represented by eight canvases, including *Still Life with Chair Caning*, and three of Braque's works were selected. Duchamp, Villon, and Gleizes were among other Cubist painters in the show. Robert Delaunay was not represented; he withdrew two other canvases after his painting *City of Paris* was turned down as too large.

Presenting hundreds of avant-garde paintings at once to an audience that had never seen nonrealistic art caused a predictable uproar. The press mocked the show and depicted it as a circus. President Theodore Roosevelt reportedly exclaimed: "That's not art!"[43] As had been the case at the French salons, the Cubist works were scorned by the majority of spectators and satirized in the press. Of the Cubists, only Villon's work proved popular, and he sold all seven of his large drypoints (a type of engraved print), which broke down forms into pyramidal planes. By contrast, Duchamp's seminal Cubist movement work, *Nude Descending a Staircase*, was singled out for ridicule more than any other out of the hundreds on display. The work created an even greater uproar in New York than it had in France. Upon seeing it, many viewers concluded that modern art was incomprehensible and ridiculous.

Nevertheless, no sooner did the Armory show's doors close than the market for modern art boomed in the United States. Collectors snatched up Cubist works as trophies, new galleries mushroomed in New York, and art dealers realized modern art was a hot commodity. Though some artists expressed concern about the new regard for modern art as a business, there was no turning back.

Italian Futurism

On the other side of the Atlantic, Duchamp's *Nude Descending a Staircase* drew the particular interest of members of an avant-garde group in Italy that had been trying to create motion in their work. Known as Futurists, the group wanted to break completely with the past and to glorify the excitement of the machine age in their art and writing. They loved speed and all modern technology, especially trains, cars, and airplanes. To create speed and movement in their art, the Futurists studied Cubist techniques to see how single forms were broken into multiple images and motion was indicated by overlapping shapes.

The Futurism movement in Italy was evident from about 1909 to 1916. Léger was one Cubist who found it a satisfactory way to portray modern industry. For most artists and critics in France, however, Futurist works were often judged by Cubist standards and found lacking. These artists failed to recognize that the two movements had different goals. While Cubism attempted to expose subjects' true structure, the Futurists seemed more concerned about expressing energy. As Apollinaire wrote somewhat disparagingly of the Futurists: "They want to paint moods."[44]

Artists who combined Cubist notions of fragmentation with the Futurist fascination with speed were known as Cubo-Futurists. The term was applied to certain works by Delaunay, Gleizes, and Metzinger as well as to works by avant-garde Russian artists such as Malevich, Natalia Goncharova, and Mikhail Larionov. Goncharova, who left Russia for Paris in 1914, founded Rayonism, which fused Cubism, Orphism, and Futurism.

Another fusion style of art inspired by Cubism and Futurism was known as Vorticism. A group of London-based artists and writers adopted the name Vorticism from the word *vortex*, or whirlpool. They were committed to capturing the energy of modern life and celebrating the machine age. They did this by employing jagged art forms that at times resembled those in Léger's Tubism. The group launched a short-lived magazine in July 1914 called *Blast*.

Cubism in Russia

Farther east and a few years earlier, at about the same time as the Blue Rider shows in Germany, the Russian public got its first glimpse of Cubism at an exhibition in Moscow in 1910–1911. Although some Russian artists were aware of

Cubism through the works of Malevich and Kandinsky as well as those by the Russian-born Sonia Delaunay and her husband, Robert, this show was the first major exhibition of the movement in Russia. It was organized by a group of artists known as the Knave of Diamonds, who had been influenced by Cézanne, Cubism, and primitivism. French Cubists were sometimes represented at the Knave of Diamonds exhibitions.

Kandinsky, the first painter to develop a totally nonrepresentational style, exhibited with the Knave of Diamonds group

Two visitors at a London auction house examine Russian painter Wassily Kandinsky's abstract work *Two Figures and Reclining Figure,* created in 1909–1910.

between 1910 and 1916. Under the influence of Cubism, his work had become increasingly abstract after 1910 while he was living in Germany. When World War I broke out, he returned to his native Russia, where his style became more geometric and began to rely almost exclusively on rectangles, circles, triangles, and squares.

Cubism and Futurism both gained large followings in Russia. Malevich, who had been deeply influenced by Léger, called himself a Cubo-Futurist. He had no desire to literally represent objects and became a leader in nonobjective art. He believed in the supremacy of abstraction and developed a pure geometric style of rectangles and squares known as Suprematism in 1913. In 1916 he published the book *From Cubism and Futurism to Suprematism.* In it he explained how square shapes

A MASTERPIECE RESTORED

Picasso's landmark canvas *Les Demoiselles d'Avignon* was sold to a private collector in 1924 and did not receive its first large-scale public exhibition until the 1937 Paris World's Fair. Soon after, it was acquired by the Museum of Modern Art and shipped to New York City, where it was first displayed in 1939.

The massive canvas—its five figures are larger than life-size—underwent a major restoration that was completed in 2004. Before starting, conservators used X-rays to study Picasso's technique of layering paint and to examine the first stages of the painting. After a thorough technical analysis, the canvas was cleaned of surface dirt, varnish, and retouching that had been done in 1950 and 1963. After the residue was removed, the painting was carefully retouched where paint had chipped away. The project returned the canvas close to its original state, allowing Picasso's vigorous brushstrokes to once again be clearly visible.

could create a superior means of expression when they represented objects. He brought together planes to create images that seemed to float in his paintings. His pure geometric style fueled a nonobjective movement that spread west from Russia toward western Europe after the war ended.

Another Russian, Liubov Popova, became a convert to Cubism after studying with Le Fauconnier and Metzinger in Paris. She became a strong follower of Braque and Picasso, but she developed her own Cubist style: Her geometric planes tended to slice into one another rather than overlap. Her shapes tilted and intersected, giving her paintings a sense of fluidity and energy. And her designs increasingly looked like objects that could actually be constructed of concrete materials, for example, *The Jug on the Table* (1915). By 1921 Popova gave up easel painting entirely to apply Cubist styles to industrial design.

Another important Russian Cubist was sculptor Alexander Archipenko. Archipenko studied painting and sculpture at the Kiev Art School before moving to Paris in 1908. There he came under the influence of the Cubists; in 1910 he began exhibiting at the Salon des Indépendants, and in 1912 joined the Section d'Or group. The Russian sculptor Vladimir Tatlin also was heavily influenced by Braque and Picasso, whose works he saw on a visit to Paris in 1913. He used some of their ideas to create assemblages. After the Russian Revolution of 1917, he and other artists and architects, including Popova, used Cubist ideas to create the movement known as Constructivism, which applied geometric design principles to all areas of life. Their goal for this movement was to make useful objects to help create an improved Russian society in the wake of the revolution.

Czech Cubism

Artists and architects in another eastern European country also focused on applying Cubism to furniture and other everyday items. In the early years of the twentieth century, the Czechoslovakian capital of Prague was recognized as an artistic center, and Cubist artists there were particularly active between 1910 and 1914. The Czech artist Frantisek Kupka, for example, was an active member of the Puteaux Group and Section d'Or.

Cubism was introduced in Prague by the art theoretician and collector Vincenc Kramar. It took root there and began to flourish, influencing both architecture and the decorative arts. Among the most original realizations of Cubist architecture are a block of Neklanova Street apartments Josef Chochol designed in 1913. Chochol and three other Czech designers —Pavel Janak, Josef Gocar, and Vlatislav Hofman—took inspiration from Braque and Picasso. The four designers believed that an object's energy could be released by breaking up the vertical and horizontal surfaces that repressed it in conventional design. They used angled planes to design objects that were works of art in their own right. In addition to cubes, they also looked to the shapes and facets of pyramids and crystals for models.

Unlike the members of the cultural establishment in other countries, traditional elites in Czechoslovakia were open to these radical ideas and supported the young designers' Cubist transformation of everything from apartment buildings to dishes. Cubist principles were applied to many office and household items, including clocks, vases, lamps, textiles, cups, saucers, and plates. In doing so, Czech artists took Cubism further than anyone else in the world yet had. A dozen totally Cubist buildings were constructed between 1911 and 1914. One of these is Prague's Czech Cubism Museum, which chronicles the unique four-year period when Czech Cubism flourished. It is housed in a Cubist building, designed by Gocar in 1912, that was originally a department store called the House of the Black Madonna.

Responses to the War

The outbreak of World War I brought changes in art communities around the world. Many artists found Cubism too tame for a war-torn world and began to pursue more radical styles

Cubist architecture, exemplified here in the stunning spiral staircase located in Prague's Museum of Czech Cubism, reached its zenith in Czechoslovakia.

In a 1952 photo, Marcel Duchamp, one of the founders of the Dadaist movement, concentrates on a chess game.

as a response to the chaos and horror of the conflict. At the outset of the war, Mondrian returned to Holland, where he cofounded De Stijl (the Style), a group that took a severely minimalist approach to art. The war, of course, had a deep impact on artists working in Germany. Franz Marc and August Macke, leaders of the Blue Rider Group, were killed at the front. Klee, who had been working in Germany, was forced to return to his native Switzerland.

Many other avant-garde artists and writers fled to neutral Switzerland during the war. There, in a Zurich cabaret called Voltaire, a group of these artists and writers, including Marcel

Duchamp, founded the movement known as Dadaism. As a response to the war, Dadaists totally rejected a rational approach to art in favor of irrationality and absurdity, which they believed better suited a world seemingly without reason and lacking human values.

Dadaism encouraged the use of chance occurrences—in fact, the group got its name from a random selection in a dictionary. It started as a literary movement in which poetry was created through a random selection of words. Art was created in a similar manner. For example, to create collage, the artist Jean Arp placed torn pieces of paper into a box, shook them up, and let them spill out. The pieces were pasted down in the pattern in which they fell. In this way, randomness and chance dictated the final composition of the picture.

Dadaism spread quickly to New York City, where Duchamp settled in 1915. He became a leader in the Dada movement in the United States and gained notoriety for his so-called ready-mades. These were works of art made out of common objects; one famous example was a urinal turned on its back, which Duchamp titled *Fountain*.

The Legacy of Cubism

Duchamp was only one of the followers of Braque and Picasso who ultimately made a total break with the tradition of representational art. While few painters remained faithful to Cubism's rigorous tenets throughout their careers, many profited from its discipline and experiments with abstraction. Although the Cubist groups were largely dispersed alter World War I, their collective break from visual realism had a profound influence on the development of art, providing a framework and new visual vocabulary that is still relevant today.

Notes

Introduction: A Revolution in Art

1. Robert Rosenblum, *Cubism and Twentieth-Century Art*. New York: Harry N. Abrams, 2001, p. 14.
2. David Cottington, *Movements in Modern Art: Cubism*. London: Tate Gallery Publishing/Cambridge University Press, 1998, p. 7.

Chapter 1: Rebelling Against Tradition: The Precursors of Cubism

3. Quoted in Raymond Cognait, *Braque*. New York: Harry N. Abrams, 1976, p. 18.
4. Quoted in Cottington, *Movements in Modern Art: Cubism*, p. 36.
5. Quoted in Patrick O'Brian, *Pablo Ruiz Picasso*. New York: G.P. Putnam's Sons, 1976, p. 152.
6. Sylvie Buisson and Christian Parisot, *Paris Montmartre: A Mecca of Modern Art, 1860–1920*. Trans. Murray Wylie. Paris: Editions Pierre Terrail, 1996, p. 150.
7. Quoted in William Rubin, *Picasso and Braque: Pioneering Cubism*. New York: Metropolitan Museum of Modern Art, 1989, p. 348.

Chapter 2: The Pioneers of Cubism: Picasso and Braque

8. Quoted in Rubin, *Picasso and Braque*, p. 354.
9. Quoted in Pierre Cabanne, *Cubism*. Paris: Editions Pierre Terrail, 2001, p. 47.
10. Quoted in Cabanne, *Cubism*, p. 48.
11. Quoted in Rubin, *Picasso and Braque*, p. 47.
12. Rubin, *Picasso and Braque*, p. 52.
13. Quoted in Rubin, *Picasso and Braque*, p. 47.
14. Quoted in Cabanne, *Cubism*, p. 31.
15. Quoted in Cabanne, *Cubism*, p. 31.
16. Quoted in Cabanne, *Cubism*, p. 28.
17. Quoted in Françoise Gilot and Carlton Lake, *Life with Picasso*. New York: McGraw-Hill, 1964, p. 74.
18. Quoted in Cabanne, *Cubism*, p. 51.
19. Quoted in Rubin, *Picasso and Braque*, p. 380.
20. Quoted in Cabanne, *Cubism*, p. 56.
21. Cottington, *Movements in Modern Art: Cubism*, p. 54.

Chapter 3: The Salon Cubists

22. Quoted in Douglas Cooper, *The Cubist Epoch*. London: Phaidon, 1970, p. 68.
23. Quoted in Rubin, *Picasso and Braque*, p. 380.

24. Quoted in Cabanne, *Cubism*, p. 48.
25. Quoted in Pierre Daix, *Cubists and Cubism*. Trans. R.F.M. Dexter. New York: Rizzoli, 1982, p. 73.
26. Quoted in Daix, *Cubists and Cubism*, p. 81.
27. Quoted in Cabanne, *Cubism*, p. 83.
28. Guillaume Apollinaire, *The Cubist Painters*. Trans. Peter Reed. East Sussex, England: Artists Bookworks, 2002, p. 17.
29. Quoted in Cabanne, *Cubism*, p. 84.
30. Quoted in Cabanne, *Cubism*, p. 84.
31. Quoted in Cottington, *Movements in Modern Art: Cubism*, p. 55.
32. Quoted in Cottington, *Movements in Modern Art: Cubism*, p. 67.
33. Quoted in Cabanne, *Cubism*, p. 96.

Chapter 4: Synthetic Cubism: Moving to Three Dimensions
34. Daix, *Cubists and Cubism*, p. 72.
35. Quoted in Cabanne, *Cubism*, p. 76.

36. Cabanne, *Cubism*, p. 122.
37. Quoted in Cabanne, *Cubism*, p. 135.
38. Gertrude Stein, *Gertrude Stein on Picasso*. New York: Liveright, 1970, p. 52.

Chapter 5: Cubism's Influence: Moving to Total Abstraction
39. Quoted in Jackie Gaff, *1910–1920: The Birth of Abstract Art*. Milwaukee: Gareth Stevens, 2001, p. 5.
40. Quoted in Cabanne, *Cubism*, p. 127.
41. Quoted in Cabanne, *Cubism*, p. 131.
42. Jim J. Jordan, *Paul Klee and Cubism*. Princeton, NJ: Princeton University Press, 1984, pp. 42–43.
43. Quoted in Leonard Diepeveen, *The Difficulties of Modernism*. New York: Routledge, 2003, p. 66.
44. Quoted in Cabanne, *Cubism*, p. 74.

For Further Reading

Books

Monica Bohm-Duchen and Janet Cook, *Understanding Modern Art*. London: Usborne, 1991. Summarizes various modern art movements and includes brief introductions to fifty-six artists from around the world.

Linda Bolton, *Art Revolutions: Cubism*. New York: Peter Bedrick, 2000. Written for young people, this book includes a brief biography of each of the important Cubist artists along with color reproductions of their work, a timeline, and a glossary.

Sylvie Buisson and Christian Parisot, *Paris Montmartre: A Mecca of Modern Art, 1860–1920*. Trans. Murray Wylie. Paris: Editions Pierre Terrail, 1996. This oversized book puts the history of Paris into an artistic context and includes many historic photographs from the Cubist era.

Pierre Cabanne, *Cubism*. Paris: Editions Pierre Terrail, 2001. The writing is fairly sophisticated, but the multitude of illustrations of Cubist works makes it a good resource for students.

Richard Muhlberger, *What Makes a Picasso a Picasso?* New York: Metropolitan Museum of Art, 1994. A simple, easy-to-understand introduction to one of the greatest artists in history and a founder of Cubism.

Laura Payne, *Essential Picasso*. Bath, UK: Parragon, 2003. This oversized book examines the life of Picasso and includes dozens of color examples of his paintings and other works during his seventy-five-year career.

Videos/DVDs

Artists of the 20th Century: Pablo Picasso. Kultur Films International, 2004. Excellent resource showing Picasso's involvement in the invention of Cubism and its Analytic and Synthetic phases.

The Impressionists. Washington, DC: New River Media. Distributed by TVF International, 1999. A helpful look at the influential period that laid the groundwork for Cubism.

Three Colors Cézanne. Chicago: Home Vision Arts, 1999. Produced by the Philadelphia Museum of Art and the British Broadcasting Corporation, this DVD is a good introduction to the artist who had the greatest impact on the Cubists and has been called the father of modern art.

Web Sites

Guggenheim Museum (Guggenheim collection.org). The official site of the Guggenheim Museum in New York City includes biographies and examples of the work of many Cubist artists.

Metropolitan Museum of Art (Metmuseum.org). The site is an excellent resource for students. A different piece of artwork is featured daily on the site, which also has a great illustrated Timeline of Art History as well as an Explore and Learn interactive section.

Museum of Modern Art (Moma.org). Includes a lot of information about Picasso since the museum owns an excellent collection of his works, including the famous *Les Demoiselles d'Avignon*. The museum's collection includes many fine Cubist works, and many are available for viewing on the Web, including works by Braque, Picasso, Gris, Léger, Robert and Sonia Delaunay, Villon, Duchamp, and Duchamp-Villon.

National Gallery of Art (nga.gov). Includes a helpful teachers' guide to art.

WebMuseum: Cubism (www.ibiblio.org /wm/paint/glo/cubism). This site makes it easy for students to become familiar with Cubist works.

Index

Picture Credits

Cover image: © 2006 Estate of Pablo Picasso/ Artists Rights Society (ARS), New York
- Pablo Picasso, "The Treble Clef." © Edimédia/CORBIS/ © Succession Picasso

Maury Aaseng (chart), 15

Abundance by Le Fauconnier, Henri Victor Gabriel (1881–1946). © Haags Gemeentemuseum, The Hague, Netherlands/The Bridgeman Art Library, 45

© Alinari Archives/CORBIS, 50

AP Images/Alastair Grant, 81

AP Images/AP Photo, 39

AP Images/Zack Seckler, 27

AP Images/Ronald Zak, 76

© 2006 Artists Rights Society (ARS), New York/ADAGP, Paris
- Georges Braque, "Homage to J.S. Bach," 1911. Homage to J.S. Bach, 1911 (oil on canvas), by Braque, Georges (1882–1963)/ © Private Collection/The Bridgeman Art Library, 36
- Georges Braque, "Houses at l'Estaque" 1908. Giraudon/Art Resource, NY, 29
- Georges Braque, "Papier Colle," 1912. Papier Colle, 1912 (collage on paper) by Braque, Georges (1882-1963)/Private Collection/Lauros/ Giraudon /The Bridgeman Art Library, 60
- Juan Gris, "Portrait of Picasso." Portrait of Pablo Picasso (1881–1973) 1912 (oil on canvas) by Gris, Juan (1887–1927) © Art Institute of Chicago, IL, USA/The Bridgeman Art Library, 40
- Fernand Léger, "Soldiers Playing at Cards," 1917. © Francis G. Mayer/ CORBIS, 68

© 2006 Artists Rights Society (ARS), New York/ADAGP, Paris/Succession Marcel Duchamp
- Marcel Duchamp, "Nude Descending a Staircase." The Philadelphia Museum of Art/Art Resource, NY, 52

© Alexander Burkatovski/CORBIS, 16

© CORBIS, 10

Eliot Elisofon/Time & Life Pictures/Getty Images, 53, 86

© 2006 Estate of Pablo Picasso / Artists Rights Society (ARS), New York
- Pablo Picasso, "Glass of Absinthe" 1914. Digital Image © The Museum of Modern Art/Licensed by Scala /Art Resource, NY, 64
- Pablo Picasso, "Guitarist," 1912. Réunion des Musées Nationaux/Art Resource, NY, 35
- Pablo Picasso, "Photo of Braque." Réunion des Musées Nationaux/Art Resource, NY, 30
- Pablo Picasso, "Still Life with Chair Caning," 1912. Réunion des Musées Nationaux/Art Resource, NY, 59
- Pablo Picasso, "Three Musicians," 1921. Digital Image © The Museum of Modern Art/Licensed by SCALA/Art Resource, NY, 70

© Geopix/Alamy, 85

© Duncan Hale-Sutton/Alamy, 73

Hulton Archive/Getty Images, 43

Erich Lessing/Art Resource, NY, 18

Mary Evans Picture Library, 15 (right image)

Réunion des Musées Nationaux / Art Resource, NY, 24

© Visual Arts Library (London)/Alamy, 9, 15 (left image), 19, 21, 23, 55

About the Author

Cynthia Mines earned a degree in English from McPherson College in Kansas and a master's degree in English from Wichita State University. She is the author of the book *For the Sake of Art*, about a Kansas art dealer instrumental in forming the famous Prairie Printmakers art group, and other books about Kansas history, and her travel articles have appeared in the *Los Angeles Times*. In 1993 she founded the arts publication *Wichita Times*.